The Documentary
Hypothesis

The Documentary Hypothesis

And the Composition of the Pentateuch

Eight Lectures
by
Umberto Cassuto

With an introduction by
Joshua A. Berman

Translated from the Hebrew by
Israel Abrahams

Shalem Press
Jerusalem and New York

Umberto Cassuto (1883–1951) held the chair of Bible studies at
the Hebrew University of Jerusalem. His books include *A Commentary on
the Book of Genesis*, *A Commentary on the Book of Exodus*, and a treatise on
Ugaritic literature entitled *The Goddess Anath*.

Shalem Press, 3 Ha'askan Street, Jerusalem
Copyright © 2006 by the Shalem Center

Fourth Printing, 2014

Originally published in Hebrew as *Torath HaTeudoth* by Magnes Press,
The Hebrew University, 1941
First English edition 1961

Cover design: Erica Halivni
Cover picture: Copyright J.L. de Zorzi/visualisrael/Corbis

ISBN 978-965-7052-35-8

Printed in Israel

∞ The paper used in this publication meets the minimum requirements of
the American National Standard for Information Sciences—Permanence of
Paper for Printed Library Materials, ANSI Z39.48-1992

CONTENTS

INTRODUCTION

We must stress, with the utmost emphasis, that there is no school of biblical scholarship today that is not founded on the critical analysis of the sources in the [Pentateuch]... and anyone who does not accept the division of the text according to the sources and the results flowing therefrom has to discharge the onus, if he wishes to be considered a collaborator in our scientific work, of proving that all the research work done till now was futile.

—Hugo Gressmann, editor,
Zeitschrift für die Alttestamentliche Wissenschaft, 1924

Rarely have such grandiose theories of origination been built and revised and pitted against one another on the evidential equivalent of the head of a pin; rarely have so many worked so long and so hard with so little to show for their trouble.

—Meir Sternberg,
The Poetics of Biblical Narrative, 1985

IN THE ENTIRE HISTORY of modern biblical scholarship, perhaps no issue has been as hotly debated as that of the origins and dating of Scripture generally and of the five books of Moses, the Pentateuch, in particular. Hugo Gressmann, a leading German biblicist and the editor of the most prestigious journal in the field of biblical studies, could indeed speak for the entire establishment of biblical scholarship in 1924 when he confidently affirmed the assumptions and findings of the Graf-Wellhausen theory of a source-critical approach to the Bible, known also as the documentary hypothesis. Yet sixty years later—and all the more so in the twenty years since then—Meir Sternberg, the author of some of the most important works in the literary analysis of Scripture, could invoke echoes of Churchill in his critique of the entire enterprise. In fairness, Sternberg's comments do not reflect the unanimous consensus of biblical scholarship—either then or even now. But it may be accurately stated that there has been a growing disaffection from historical paradigms of biblical study. And while one still routinely sees references to the putative sources J, E, P, and D, some have wondered aloud whether Wellhausen's construct has begun to show enough cracks and strains to place its own survival in doubt.[1]

This brief essay, written on the 65th anniversary of the original publication of *The Documentary Hypothesis*, is an attempt to take a page from the history of ideas and trace the stated and unstated beliefs that have guided biblical scholars in their work over the past century. It is a journey through what Thomas Kuhn famously characterized as a "paradigm shift,"[2] a shift in biblical studies whose pivotal figure, nearly without rival, is that of the Italian-born Umberto Cassuto (1883–1951), who laid out his program in this short treatise.

A brief recapitulation of Kuhn's theory concerning the nature of scientific inquiry is instructive in understanding the place of *The Documentary Hypothesis* within the spectrum of biblical scholarship. A mature science, according to Kuhn's hypothesis, is one in which there exists a dominant paradigm—a conceptual framework that informs the scientist of what to expect as he engages in his or her scientific inquiry. It delineates the parameters of what can and cannot be considered acceptable solutions to a problem.

Only that which conforms to the paradigm is deemed true. The training of scientists consists of inculcating them with the tenets of the paradigm, the rules of the game, before they embark on their own research. To engage in "normal science" is to endeavor to tie up loose ends and adjust the paradigm to reality. Paradigms introduce a sociological factor into science. To practice science is to engage the mysteries of the natural order not in unmediated fashion, but through the lens of the paradigm, itself a human construct. This dogmatic aspect determines who is considered "in" in the scientific community, and who is "out."

Inevitably, results will begin to arise that are inconsistent with the reigning paradigm. At first these will be dismissed and faults will be found either with the method employed or with the assumptions upon which they rest. As these bothersome findings persist and accumulate, however, a creative scientist will come forward to challenge the axioms of the paradigm and propose a new one that encompasses the "problematic" results as well in a systematic fashion. Because the old paradigm is but a human construct, it is subject to human foibles: its articulators will typically dig in their heels, and the new paradigm will gain traction only as the masters of the old one pass from the scene. New paradigms do gain influence, but only slowly.

The notion that the received text of the Pentateuch had a pre-history that consisted of smaller, earlier documents had been in currency in France and Germany since the mid-eighteenth century. Scholars had hypothesized about the existence of these documents on the basis of apparent duplications, repetitions, and contradictions. But the theories advanced before Wellhausen (1844–1918) had been piecemeal. Only his *Prolegomena to the History of Israel* (1876) seemed to account for all the phenomena observed.[3] Unlike earlier theories, Wellhausen's purported to explain the entirety of the Pentateuch. It offered clear parameters for determining how a given passage could be reliably assigned to a particular source document. Above all, it supplied a rationale for the entire edifice, tracing the historical evolution of the received text. Each of four source documents, he claimed, reflected a distinct stage not only in the development of the text but, more importantly, in the development of the religion of ancient Israel. Each document, asserted Wellhausen, was originally a full and independent account of the history of Israel, from its earliest beginnings through the time of Moses. The J document, the earliest of the four, was the account that had been formulated by scribes of the court of Judea. The E document had been produced by their rivals in the northern kingdom. Following the fall of Samaria in the late eighth century B.C.E., Wellhausen surmised, a redactor had melded the two accounts. The D document, comprising most of the Book of Deuteronomy, had been composed by scribes in Judea in the time of Josiah, toward the close of the First Temple period in the late seventh or early sixth century B.C.E. The P document had been authored by Temple priests early on in the Second Temple era following the return from exile (late sixth to early fifth centuries B.C.E.). Each document, claimed Wellhausen, was characterized by its own theology, politics, language, and style.

The theory was quickly adopted by biblical scholars everywhere, attaining the status of a paradigm. One is reminded of Hugo Gressmann's contention cited at the outset of this essay (and taken from the opening chapter of the present volume), that one had to accept this theory in order to be "considered a collaborator in our scientific work." Indeed, in the generation following Wellhausen, scholars labored nearly exclusively to tie up loose ends—sharpening the criteria for assigning the various Pentateuchal passages to the four documents, altering the dating and precise chronology of each document, and reviewing whether a given passage should be attributed to this document or that.

The greatest advance in biblical scholarship in the generation after Wellhausen took place within the paradigm of the documentary hypothesis. Hermann Gunkel spearheaded an attempt to get at what he considered the oral roots of the pentateuchal passages and to locate their original social function in the daily cultic and royal life of ancient Israel. In essence, Gunkel took Wellhausen's assumptions about sources one step further. Wellhausen had maintained that the Pentateuch could be reduced to four sources. Gunkel splintered these into dozens more.

In the present work, originally published in Hebrew in 1941 and presented here in accordance with Israel Abrahams' 1961 translation, Cassuto acknowledges that his counter-theory represents a challenge to the existing paradigm. He notes that at its inception, Wellhausen's idea had been cautiously regarded as a "theory" or a "hypothesis," with the tentativeness inherent in those terms. Cassuto decries the fact that "its original character had been entirely forgotten, and that a kindly fate had saved it from being mortal like other scientific hypotheses." Instead, it now bore the venerable status of an imposing edifice, in which proud attendants continue to "build and perfect it, and are still busy decorating its halls and completing its turrets." (p. 117) Upheld dogmatically by its practitioners, and serving as the measure of who could be considered a true biblicist and who not, the documentary hypothesis was indeed a paradigm in the harshest sense of the word. Cassuto's experience attests that those who first challenged the hypothesis were quickly dismissed. Certainly, it was claimed in defense, a slight weakness in the theory here or there was insufficient to relegate the entire doctrine to the dustbin. Moreover, detractors could be easily dispensed with because they proposed no alternative to explain the data at hand.

Herein lies the significance of Cassuto's work. A distillation of the author's first major work, *La Questione della Genesi*,[4] published in 1934, *The Documentary Hypothesis* attacked its subject on multiple fronts. Moreover, it offered an alternative approach to the phenomena the source critics had observed. The key, suggested Cassuto, was to reject the assumptions of source criticism entirely and to articulate "a new edifice that is to be built in place of the old, collapsed structure"—in short, a new paradigm for biblical studies. Cassuto proposed that the increasing atomization and fragmentation of the biblical text be reversed. Instead, the Pentateuch had to be construed as a carefully constructed whole. It needed to be mined for the deliberate choice of each expression. What had been construed as contradiction, repetition, and variance were in fact literary tools succinctly conveying polyphonous meaning. Cassuto saw within the Torah the literary devices of harmony, word play, assonance and consonance, elliptic and dramatic structure, and retrospection.[5] He accepted the observations of source criticism, that the text exhibited phenomena that begged explanation. His close readings of the text as a well-integrated whole were, in his estimation, not merely an alternative approach to Scripture. Rather, they more fully and consistently accounted for the very phenomena that the source critics themselves had sought to explain. In a sentence, Cassuto represents a pivotal figure in the paradigm shift in modern biblical studies from source criticism to literary criticism. The transition has been slow, however, with literary analysis of the Bible beginning to flourish within the halls of academia only in the 1970s.

Cassuto's critique of the documentary hypothesis was grounded in his knowledge of ancient Near Eastern languages and literature—a corpus of material publicized largely after Wellhausen had drafted his thesis. For example, Cassuto argued, the variation in divine names within a single work was commonplace in the literature of the biblical period. Similarly, whereas source critics had assumed that authors of all ages would never digress and would neither repeat nor contradict themselves, Cassuto demonstrated that these

premises imposed canons of modern literary convention upon bod-
ies of literature to which they were entirely foreign. Indeed, it has
since been shown that many phenomena that were fodder for the
source critics have emerged in the Temple scroll found at Qumran,
a work universally attributed to a single author.

Cassuto also questions one of the weakest aspects of the documentary hypothesis: the role of the four redactors it proposed
and the hermeneutics that purportedly guided their work. Most
significantly, he notes that when a particular divine name appears
out of place in a document, the source critics failed to see this
anomaly as a flaw in their theory. The documents, they insisted,
are always consistent; the "wrong" name, then, must be the work
of a careless redactor, and the text should be amended to reflect
the intent of the original author.[6]

Photographs of Cassuto in his study are indicative of the breadth
of European culture that he brought to his scholarship. Here we
see a man impeccably dressed in a three-piece suit and tie, peering
through round spectacles over a finely waxed mustache, its two
ends curled to full crescents. Born in Florence in 1883, Cassuto
received a state education from primary school through university, mastering the languages and literatures of Greek and Latin,
French and Italian, English and German—resources he brings to
bear in this work, as seen in his frequent references to Dante's
Divine Comedy. Indeed, his students note that in his final lecture,
before his sudden demise in December of 1951, he elucidated the
doubled stories of the Book of Numbers through analogy with
those in medieval French epic poetry.[7]

This breadth of knowledge, in turn, contributed to the depth
of Cassuto's analysis. The highlight of the opening lecture of this
work, for example, is his observation that the evolution of source

criticism in nineteenth-century biblical scholarship parallels developments within Homeric studies. Thus, he claimed, "it may well be that we have before us not an objective discovery of what is actually to be found in the ancient books, but the result of the subjective impression that these writings have on the people of a given environment." (p. 15) "The mode of the period and country clearly stamped the labors of the scholars." (p. 12)

Subsequent scholars have noted just how true this assessment is of the conditioned and tendentious underpinnings of Wellhausen's theory. Reflecting upon his own work, Wellhausen wrote in 1901 that "our vital concern is research without presuppositions; research that does not find what it is supposed to find according to considerations of purpose and relevance, but what seems correct to the conscientious researcher from a logical and historical point of view."[8] But the cultural subsoil of the documentary hypothesis is today revealed. Its first layer is a tendency characteristic of the nineteenth and early twentieth centuries to delineate the development and evolution of trends. For Darwin, nature was not a unified whole, but dynamic throughout history. For Freud, the human psyche was not immutable from birth to death, but subject to conflict and struggle played out over time. For both these thinkers, change was of the essence, and a proper understanding of the sequence of things was vital to understanding the object of study. Hence, for Wellhausen, it was crucial not only to posit multiple source documents but to see them as reflections of distinct theological stages of Israel's religious development. This is why we find within Wellhausen's theory not only the claim of distinct documents, but a broad explanation of their historical sequence and historical setting.[9]

Coupled with Wellhausen's historicist orientation was a strong romanticist streak. For romanticism, every cultural phenomenon has a primitive phase analogous to childhood, a classical phase analogous to adulthood, and a decadent phase analogous to senility. Thus, for Wellhausen, E was a theological advance over the earlier, more primitive J. These texts were thought to reflect spontaneity and spirit, bearing out the romanticist belief that the primitive is the most sublime. By contrast, the work of the priests, P, the latest of the purported documents, was taken to mark a decadent stage in the religion of Israel, with its attention to ritual laws.[10]

The rise of alternative paradigms and a growing awareness of the documentary hypothesis' nineteenth-century ideological assumptions have led many scholars to disaffection with it. There is less and less consensus about the criteria for identifying each of the documents. In some circles, the P document is actually composed of seven P sub-documents. John Van Seters has recently demonstrated that the very notion of a redactor of the type Wellhausen envisioned is anachronistic; such redactors belong only to the age of print.[11] The trickle of comparative materials from the ancient Near East that were available to Wellhausen were never employed in the formulation of the theory. As that trickle has become a torrent, it has become evident that numerous hermeneutical assumptions of the source critics about consistency, redundancy, and repetition simply did not hold sway in the ancient Near East. Thus, today we are acutely aware of the nineteenth-century intellectual and literary currents that informed Wellhausen's work. For many in the field, the effort to critically and scientifically refract the sources of the Pentateuch from its received whole is the textual equivalent of attempting to unscramble an egg.

But we have told only half the story. Apart from being a learned scholar, Cassuto was also an ordained rabbi, having served as the chief rabbi of Florence and the head of its rabbinic seminary from 1922 to 1925. Though Cassuto does not say so explicitly, the paradigm shift he wrought bore a subtext of Jewish-Christian polemics. To understand this shift, we need to understand source criticism's strong affinities with a sometimes anti-Semitic Protestant theology. Solomon Schechter famously equated "higher criticism" with "higher anti-Semitism,"[12] and one can indeed find anti-Jewish references in *The Prolegomena*. One example concerns the last eight chapters of First Chronicles, detailing David's efforts to procure materials for the construction of the First Temple under Solomon. In one particularly grievous comment on these chapters, Wellhausen writes, "1 Chr. 22-29 is a startling instance of that statistical phantasy of the Jews which revels in vast sums of money on paper."[13] But, by and large, this is not the tone of *The Prolegomena*, and it would be a mistake to categorize it as an anti-Semitic manifesto. Yet the underpinnings of Wellhausen's hypothesis may be seen to have an affinity with Protestant theology in at least three ways.

Long before Wellhausen, eighteenth- and nineteenth-century scholars considered the laws of the Pentateuch to be material whose composition was early relative to the other documents. Yet Wellhausen assigned these ordinances to the post-exilic period. This material included the P document, extending from Exodus 25 through the beginning of the Book of Numbers and dealing largely, though not exclusively, with cultic matters. In the introduction to *The Prolegomena*, he explains:

> It was in vain that I looked for the light which was to be shed from this source [i.e., the laws] on the historical and prophetic books. On the contrary, my enjoyment of the latter was marred by the Law; it did not bring them any nearer to me, but intruded itself uneasily, like a ghost that makes a noise, but is not visible and really effects nothing.... At last, in the course of a casual visit in Göttingen in the summer of 1867, I learned that... Karl Heinrich Graf placed the Law later than the Prophets, and almost without knowing his reasons for the hypothesis, I was prepared to accept it.[14]

We see here the full implications of Wellhausen's romanticist orientation, whereby the last stage of a cultural phenomenon represents its final decline, much like aged infirmity in a human being. For Wellhausen, the spirit and good acts of the prophets are to be celebrated. By contrast, the laws vital for the structuring and ordering of community are relics of the Israelite religion's decadent phase. This Pauline antinomian bias favors spirit over law and universalism over the sectarian community.[15]

A second affinity between the documentary hypothesis and Christian theology lies in the resemblance it yields between the Pentateuch (now reduced from five books to four documents) and the four evangelical Gospels of the New Testament. Recall that for Wellhausen, J, E, P, and D are not merely original sources of the Pentateuch. Rather, each represents its own version of the entire history of Israel, from Creation to Moses. Put differently, according to the documentary hypothesis, both the Pentateuch and the Gospels contain four accounts of the foundational history of a religion. Could it be that these German scholars of the Old Testament—most of whom were also scholars of the New Testament—had applied the religious training they had received regarding the ways in which the Old Testament presaged the New to the problem of the Old Testament's origins? It is worth noting in this vein that very few stories or even archetypes of stories in the Pentateuch appear even three times, let alone four. It has also been pointed out that source critics assign virtually no patriarchal narratives in the Pentateuch to the putative E document.[16] The insistence, therefore, that the four documents were originally four versions of the history of Israel could very well have some roots in the New Testament's four Gospels attesting to the historical life of Jesus.

Thirdly, one should note the diminished status of the biblical text for some strands of Protestant theology. For classical Jewish theology, the Masoretic text represents the revealed, immutable word of God. Yet for Christianity generally, no accepted, fixed canonical text reflects the original language of composition of the New Testament, be it Aramaic, Greek, or Hebrew. In other words, Christians do not view the New Testament as the direct word of God. The Gospels are considered holy because they attest to the miracle of Christ. To engage the Gospels, then, is to read through the text to something beyond it: the life of Christ. The text merely points to that. Hence, Christianity can accept criticism of the biblical text, for the text itself is not of ultimate significance.

It is not surprising, therefore, that liberal Protestant theologians entertained similar views of the Old Testament. One such thinker was Charles Augustus Briggs, co-author of the classic Brown-Driver-Briggs ("BDB") biblical lexicon, composed a century ago, and a Presbyterian minister and lecturer at Union Theological Seminary. In 1901, Briggs addressed the theological importance of source criticism for the faithful:

> The valleys of biblical truth have been filled up with the debris of human dogmas, ecclesiastical institutions, liturgical formulas, priestly ceremonies, and casuistic practices. Historical criticism is searching for the rock-bed of divine truth and the massive foundations of the Divine Word, in order to recover the real Bible. Historical criticism is sifting all this rubbish. It will gather our every precious stone. Nothing will escape its keen eye.[17]

For this theologian source criticism hardly threatens religious faith; it actually serves it. The text is not inherently holy; it only points to what is. The believer is challenged to read through the text and, through the layers of its pre-history, to arrive at that which is authentic and meaningful.

It should come as no surprise, then, that the earliest major academic assaults on the documentary hypothesis came from two traditional Jewish scholars, Umberto Cassuto and Benno Jacob.[18] Both objected to the documentary hypothesis even as they eschewed

Mosaic composition of the Pentateuch. Their opposition to the hypothesis was not rooted in adherence to doctrinal orthodoxy. In proposing a paradigm shift toward a system of analysis that focused on the unity of the text, however, they espoused a new paradigm that may be demonstrated to be fundamentally Jewish in orientation.

For classical rabbinic Judaism, the biblical text itself is the vehicle of revelation, and every word is therefore holy and immutable. Cassuto does not spell out his theology, but he seems to have regarded the Torah as a divinely inspired whole, even if not composed by Moses, and even if it comprises and reworks pre-existing sources. In any case, the paradigm he lays out here is rooted in the rabbinic tradition in which he was so steeped—a tradition that took the unity of the Torah as axiomatic. The source critics, by contrast, saw the earlier sources to be the only context in which the final form of the text before us makes any sense. Thus, a later redactor's erasure of the boundaries between the original texts was to be lamented.

It is important to note that Christian theology was not monolithic on this point during the twentieth century. For theologians like Francis Watson, following Karl Barth, the fact of erasure of boundaries between original texts is affirmed but hardly lamented. In Watson's view, the original sources were intentionally reworked in an act of welcome inspiration. Rather than dwelling on the prehistory of the received text, these theologians celebrate the creation of a text designed to fulfill its canonical mission as a vehicle through which to impart the divine message.[19]

In a Jewish context, this conception of Scripture as an organic whole, even as the ideology of Mosaic authorship is rejected, was shared by Franz Rosenzweig. Source critics referred to the putative editor of Scripture as "R," for redactor, but Rosenzweig took the liberty of appropriating this shorthand as a reference to *rabbeinu*, our teacher. By this device, he meant that the finished product before us is to be viewed organically, with any putative editing being part of an overarching design, not the piecemeal stitching together of disparate texts.

Cassuto's emphasis on the unity of the Torah and on its variation and repetition as vehicles to convey shades of meaning has Jewish roots elsewhere as well. Yaakov Elman has noted that while classical Jewish commentators had always revered the biblical text, the status of the biblical text and the nature of their exegesis took a decided turn in the nineteenth century.[20] It is not uncommon, Elman claims, to find medieval exegetes unbothered by biblical repetition or use of synonyms to refer to the same entity in different ways.[21] In the nineteenth century, however, the rise of radical Reform Judaism and of biblical criticism impelled a whole new age of Orthodox biblical exegetes to safeguard the sanctity of Scripture. This mission prompted an exegetical search for what Elman and others term "omnisignificance"—the quest for comprehensible significance even in slight variations and synonyms in the text. Highly close readings in this vein are legion in the commentaries of Samson Raphael Hirsch, Yaakov Zvi Mecklenberg, and Meir Lubish Malbim, to name several. Cassuto was quite familiar with these commentators, and their predilection toward omnisignificance may have led him to adduce a program of exegesis that assumed the integrity and unity of the text as an irreducible document in which every detail could be mined for meaning.

One school of contemporary epistemology, often associated with Hans Georg Gadamer, maintains that all understanding, whether of history, art, or the Bible, is attainable only within a tradition. A tradition imbues its sons with a conceptual framework and interpretive horizons. A tradition provides its adherents with the questions to be asked of a text, which in turn allows the text to answer those questions within the framework of the tradition. For

Cassuto, the source critical approach represented a paradigm of analysis fraught with hermeneutical assumptions that were utterly foreign to him. *The Documentary Hypothesis* represents an alternative paradigm of biblical analysis, whose fundamental terms are much more in accord with traditional Jewish assumptions about the nature of the received biblical text.

A lifelong Zionist, Cassuto arrived in Jerusalem in 1939 to take up a post as a professor of biblical studies at the Hebrew University, after discriminatory laws in Italy necessitated his emigration. In his inaugural address, he spoke passionately about the role rigorous biblical study could play in the renaissance of the Jewish people in its ancestral homeland. He concluded with a prayer:

> Just as the books of Scripture proved a source of blessing for our forefathers, may it be so too for us, for our children and our children's children. May they raise our spirits and embolden our hearts to realize our aspirations and to achieve the aims toward which we have directed our being, the renewal of the people of Israel upon the Land of Israel.[22]

Yet Cassuto's blessing, expressed in that fateful year of 1939, would not be fully granted for his own children and his children's children. In 1945, his only son, Rabbi Dr. Nathan Cassuto, was deported by the Germans and put to death in a concentration camp. His daughter-in-law, who subsequently emigrated to Israel, was murdered in the ambush of a convoy to Mount Scopus in 1948. Inspired by their *pater familias*, David Cassuto and the other surviving members of the Cassuto family in Israel have set themselves to the task of assembling an archive of his writings. I am indebted to them for their assistance in the preparation of this essay. Perhaps the republication of this volume after nearly half a century can in some small way perpetuate the legacy of its author, in the spirit of the prophet Isaiah (56:5), as an "everlasting name that shall not perish."

Joshua A. Berman
Jerusalem
December 2005/Kislev 5766

NOTES

1. The state of the discussion is summarized in Joseph Blenkinsopp, *The Pentateuch: An Introduction to the First Five Books of the Bible* (New York: Doubleday, 1992), p. viii.

2. Thomas S. Kuhn, *The Structure of Scientific Revolutions* (Chicago: University of Chicago Press, 1970).

3. Julius Wellhausen, *Prolegomena zur Geschichte Israels* (Berlin: Reimer, 1876); *Prolegomena to the History of Israel*, trans. J. Sutherland Black and Allan Menzies under the author's supervision, preface by W. Robertson Smith, foreword by Douglas A. Knight (Atlanta: Scholars Press, 1994).

4. *La Questione della Genesi* (Florence: F. Le Monnier, 1934), published in Hebrew as *Sefer Bereshit U-mivnehu*, trans. M.E. Hartom (Jerusalem: Magnes Press, 1990). For a full bibliography of Cassuto's writings, see S.E. Loewenstamm, ed., *Studies in Bible Dedicated to the Memory of U. Cassuto on the 100th Anniversary of His Birth* (Jerusalem: Magnes Press, 1987), pp. 9-42. [Hebrew]

5. For a full analysis of Cassuto's exegetical style, see Moshe Yitzhaki, "The Desired and Actual Approach to Biblical Scholarship in the Eyes of M.D. Cassuto," *Beit Mikra* 15 (1970), pp. 327-338. [Hebrew]

6. Since Cassuto's day, the critique of the documentary hypothesis has expanded in many directions. See Roger Norman Whybray, *The Making of the Pentateuch: A Methodological Study* (Sheffield: Journal for the Study of the Old Testament Press, 1987).

7. Alexander Rofé, "Moshe David Cassuto: The Impressions of the Youngest of His Students," *Beit Mikra* 30:2 (1985), p. 237. [Hebrew]

8. *Universitätsunterricht und Konfession* (Berlin, 1901), p. 153, quoted in John Barton, "Wellhausen's *Prolegemona to the History of Israel*: Influences and Effects," in Daniel Smith Christopher, ed., *Text & Experience: Towards a Cultural Exegesis of the Bible* (Sheffield: Sheffield Academic Press, 1995), p. 326.

9. Jon Douglas Levenson, "Response to Edward L. Greenstein, 'Biblical Studies in a State,'" in Shaye J.D. Cohen and Edward L. Greenstein, eds., *The State of Jewish Studies* (Detroit: Wayne State University Press, 1990), pp. 47-48.

10. Barton, "Wellhausen's *Prolegomena*," p. 326.

11. John Van Seters, "An Ironic Circle: Wellhausen and the Rise of Redaction Criticism," *Zeitschrift für die Alttestamentliche Wissenschaft* 115 (2003), pp. 487-500.

12. Solomon Schechter, "Higher Criticism—Higher Anti-Semitism," in Solomon Schechter, *Seminary Addresses and Other Papers* (1st ed. 1915; New York: Arno Press, 1969), pp. 35-39.

13. Wellhausen, *Prolegomena*, p. 181.

14. Wellhausen, *Prolegomena*, pp. 3-4. See also Romans 7:7-11.

15. Jon Douglas Levenson, *The Hebrew Bible, the Old Testament, and Historical Criticism: Jews and Christians in Biblical Studies* (Louisville: Westminster John Knox Press, 1993), p. 12.

16. See discussion in Whybray, *The Making of the Pentateuch*, p. 28.

17. C.A. Briggs, *General Introduction to the Study of Holy Scripture* (New York, 1901), p. 531, quoted in James Kugel, "Bible Studies and Jewish Studies," *AJS Newsletter* 36 (1986), p. 23.

18. On the scholarship of the German Jewish scholar Benno Jacob (1862–1945), see the anthology of essays in German and in English by Walter Jacob and Almuth Jürgensen, *Die Exegese hat das erste Wort: Beiträge zu Leben und Werk Benno Jacobs* (Stuttgart: Calwer Verlag, 2002). Jacob's work bears many lines of affinity with Cassuto's in terms of looking at the text as a structured, unified whole with subtle, literary nuances. Cassuto and Jacob corresponded in 1929 and met while the latter was in transit, in Rome in 1934.

19. Francis Watson, *Text, Church and World: Biblical Interpretation in Theological Perspective* (Grand Rapids, MI: Eerdmans, 1994), p. 40.

20. Yaakov Elman, "Benno Jacob in Historical Context," in Jacob and Jürgensen, *Die Exegese hat das erste Wort*, pp. 113-114.

21. See, for example, Ibn Ezra on Exodus 20:1.

22. Umberto Cassuto, "Our Task in Biblical Studies," in *Biblical and Canaanite Literatures* (Jerusalem: Magnes Press, 1972), p. 11. [Hebrew]

TRANSLATOR'S NOTE

DESPITE THE PASSAGE OF TIME, this little volume (which is now rendered for the first time from Hebrew into English) remains a classic in the field of biblical studies. Though summary in form and popular in presentation, it provides a masterly exposition of the documentary hypothesis and subjects its exegetical methods and conclusions to a critical probe that is distinguished alike by brilliant scholarship and acute textual analysis. The writer challenges the widely held theory that the Pentateuch is an amalgam of fragments excised from various source-documents of different authorship, date, style and outlook. He examines the basic arguments of the prevailing higher critical view one by one, and proceeds to rebut them with compelling logic supported by profound learning. The result is not so much a scientific edifice laid in ruins as the reaffirmation of the Torah's literary and artistic integrity and the enhancement of its spiritual significance.

But a note of warning must be sounded. It is axiomatic that every literary work must be approached in the light of the author's intention. It would obviously be an absurdity to read a lyric poem as though it were a scientific essay, or to judge a novel by the criteria of a documented history. This principle of criticism, *mutatis mutandis*, must also be observed in assessing the value of the present volume.

The Documentary Hypothesis was originally compiled as a course of lectures for schoolteachers who had only a superficial acquaintance with the theories of biblical higher criticism. As a gifted pedagogue, the late Professor Cassuto knew how to adapt the presentation of his subject to his audience. The spoken word, he realized, is governed by different stylistic requirements from those of the written exposition; moreover, the full use of the panoply of technical data and arguments, which the scholar employs in a scientific dissertation, was ruled out by the limitations of time and the restricted knowledge of his listeners in this branch of study.

The author accordingly gave a popular form to his discourses; he couched his thoughts in an easy, conversational style, and made ample use of simile and metaphor with a view to maintaining the unflagging interest of his students. His illustrations are invariably apt and telling; and he does not hesitate on occasion to drive his contention home with a parable. Throughout he has avoided overwhelming the beginner with a spate of confusing detail. Instead he refers the enthusiast, who wishes to delve more deeply into the subject, to scholarly works where he can find a fuller discussion of the questions. In particular he draws attention to his own comprehensive treatise on the problems of Genesis, *La Questione della Genesi*. That in the end the learned professor was requested to publish his lectures is not surprising; nor can one dispute the wisdom of his decision (explained in his Preface) to retain the lecture character of these discourses in their published form. Any other course would have involved writing an entirely new book.

It would be a grave mistake, however, to equate popularization with lack of scientific qualities. The literary framework of this epitome of Cassuto's views on the documentary theory may represent a concession to the layman; but the content—the argument and critical analysis—is based on sound reasoning and vast erudition, fully elaborated in the writer's larger Italian book. The brevity and clarity of this little work will undoubtedly commend it to the general reader; and the scholar, it is believed, will likewise find this volume of significance. It is not only an excellent summary of the author's earlier publications, but it also contains, as we learn from the Preface, some additional material dispersed over its pages. Altogether *The Documentary Hypothesis* serves as a valuable introduction to the late Professor Cassuto's Hebrew commentaries on the Pentateuch, which have helped so much to illumine our understanding of Scripture with the light of new knowledge and interpretation, expounded by one of the most original minds among modern biblical exegetes.

I would conclude by expressing my increasing sense of gratitude to Professor Benjamin Mazar and Mr. Silas S. Perry for their continuing encouragement and support, without which this translation would not have seen the light of day. I wish also to record my indebtedness to Dr. M. Cassuto-Salzmann for her many valuable suggestions and for the painstaking care with which she read the proofs and prepared the indexes. Her work was inspired throughout by true filial devotion. Finally, I should like to record my indebtedness to Dr. M. Spitzer for his invaluable advice on the format and printing of this work, which he gave with unfailing courtesy and fine aesthetic understanding.

Israel Abrahams
Cape Town
January 1960/Teveth 5720

TRANSLITERATION KEY

(a) CONSONANTS

א	=	ʾ	ל	=	l
בּ	=	b	מ, ם	=	m
ב	=	bh	נ, ן	=	n
גּ	=	g	ס	=	s
ג	=	gh	ע	=	ʿ
דּ	=	d	פּ	=	p
ד	=	dh	פ, ף	=	ph
ה	=	h	צ, ץ	=	ṣ
ו	=	w	ק	=	q
ז	=	z	ר	=	r
ח	=	ḥ	שׂ	=	ś
ט	=	ṭ	שׁ	=	š
י	=	y	תּ	=	t
כּ	=	k	ת	=	th
כ, ך	=	kh			

Note: (1) Unsounded ה at the end of a word is not represented in the transcription;
(2) the customary English spelling is retained for biblical names, e.g., Isaac, Esau.

(b) VOWELS

Long				Short		
⸳ (*Qāmeṣ gādhōl*)	=	ā		-	=	a
⸳⸳ ,ׅ (*Ḥīreq gādhōl*)	=	ī		⸱	=	e
⸳ , ⸳⸳	=	ē		· (*Ḥīreq qāṭān*)	=	i
⸳⸳⸳ , ו	=	ō		⸳ (*Qāmeṣ qāṭān*)	=	o
ו	=	ū		⸜	=	u

⸱ (*Šᵉwā*)	=	e̠
⸗	=	ă
⸗	=	ŏ
⸗	=	ĕ

Note: Capital E represents ⸗, ⸗ and ⸗; thus אֱלֹהִים is transliterated *'Elōhīm*, and אֵל is transcribed *'El*.

ABBREVIATIONS

E = Elohist   P = Priestly Code
J = Jahwist   D = Deuteronomic Code

The Documentary Hypothesis

PREFACE

THE LECTURES THAT I NOW PRESENT to the public were originally composed for the teachers' post-graduate courses held in the summer of 1940 in Jerusalem. At the conclusion of these courses, many of the teachers who had attended approached me with the request that I should publish this series of lectures, and thus make it easier for them to review the subject when they so desired; at the same time those who had not heard my discourses would be able to study them in printed form. I readily agreed, and I immediately prepared the lectures for publication. I regret that for reasons beyond my control the printing was delayed until now, and that only after the lapse of more than a year has the book been able to make its appearance.

The subject which this volume treats has occupied me a long time. When I was working on my lectures on the Pentateuch, and more particularly on the Book of Genesis, which I delivered in the State University of Florence from the academic year 1925–26 onward, I began to realize that the prevailing theories do not provide a complete and wholly satisfactory solution to the difficulties and problems arising from an investigation of the biblical text. This has prompted me to re-examine these difficulties and problems independently on the basis of a detached and exact textual study. To this task I devoted first a series of essays in Italian, Hebrew and German, and ultimately a comprehensive and voluminous work in Italian, which was published in 1934, under the auspices of the University of Florence and with the assistance of the Italian Academy.[1] I am now compiling a second edition of that book in Hebrew, but the task of revising the material will undoubtedly take some time; hence it seems to me that it will not be superfluous, in the meantime, to publish this small volume, which provides a summary of the Italian work, and contains, needless to say—since there is no research without discovery—some new material here and there.

Having composed this synopsis in the first instance as a series of lectures, I am now publishing it in the same form. I purposely refrained from obscuring its original character, because it appeared to me that it was precisely the lecture form that was most suited to a book of this kind, which does not aim to place before professional scholars the detailed researches of the author, but to explain to the general public, in an easy and simple manner, the essence of the subject. It is as though I came now to address the public and to repeat to them what I had told the teachers last year. For this reason, I have not included in this book references, or detailed notes, or anything of the usual scientific apparatus; all this will be found in the Italian volume and can be consulted there. However, I have not conceded one iota, I need hardly stress, in regard to the scientific character of the content; the scholarly apparatus is not visible, but in actuality it constitutes the foundation of my entire dissertation.

Although I avoided loading this handbook with notes and the like, I thought it right to add at the end a short bibliography for the guidance of those readers who would like to study the subject more deeply.

Since this volume is only a popular digest of a comprehensive scientific work, it is self-understood that not everything that can be said on the matters discussed is stated explicitly. Consequently if the reader should find something difficult to understand, he is kindly asked to refer, if possible, to my Italian work, where he may find the answer to his question.

I venture to hope that this publication may serve to focus attention on the important subject to which it is devoted, and inspire a greater desire on the part of the *Yishuv* [Palestine Jewish community] to engage in the scientific study of the Bible without any bias or preconceived ideas, but only with the object of seeking the truth and understanding the scriptural text thoroughly.

U. Cassuto
Jerusalem
August 1941/Elul 5701

THE DOCUMENTARY HYPOTHESIS
AND ITS CRITERIA

ONE OF THE MOST important attributes of science is its per-
petual restlessness. It is constantly developing, changing its aspect,
transforming and renewing itself, expanding and progressing without surcease. Its victories and conquests are but starting points for
fresh triumphs, and its achievements form the preparatory bases
for new attainments. The structures that it builds for itself with
stones quarried by analysis and arranged architectonically by synthesis—resplendent palaces of the human intellect—are not destined
to endure forever. They permit us to gaze from their rooftops and
through their windows upon the area stretching in front of them
and upon the road leading forward, and they serve as lighthouses
that illumine this path before us. But sometimes it happens that
one of these edifices, which for a given period was distinguished
for its strength and stability and its capacity to withstand ordinary winds and even extraordinary storms, begins, in the course
of time, to totter and inclines to fall, be it because the ground
on which it was erected was not sufficiently solid, or because
the stones of its walls and pillars were not hewn from enduring
rock, or because the work of the builders was not done well, or

for all these reasons together. Then it behooves us to abandon the building and to continue our way forward until we succeed in finding a fitting site on which to establish a new structure in place of the old.

Such cases are daily occurrences in the history of science. To one example, which is taking place now in biblical scholarship, I propose to devote the series of lectures that I commence to deliver to you today. Concepts that until a few decades ago, that up to about twenty years ago—possibly even less—were regarded as permanent achievements of scholarship, as conclusions that were completely unchallengeable, have now begun to crumble before the criticism levelled at them, and appear in part dubious and in part completely erroneous. A structure that seemed to be one of the unassailable postulates of science has begun to show signs of disintegration; and even in the circle of the architects and builders who erected it an element of doubt is manifesting itself concerning its future existence. This is the present position in regard to the most vital questions in biblical scholarship, its fundamental problems, which are concerned with the origin and composition of the books of the Pentateuch.

Until recently, the doctrine known as the Theory of Documents was counted among the strongest edifices of science.[1] Although it was still designated a "theory" as at the time of its formulation, it seemed as if this, its original character, had been entirely forgotten, and that a kindly fate had saved it from being mortal like other scientific hypotheses. There was not a scholar who doubted that the Torah was compiled in the period of the Second Temple from various documents or sources: one source was J (Jahwist), which used the name YHWH from the beginning of the story of Creation; another source was E (Elohist), according to which the Tetragrammaton was first revealed to Moses, and hence it employed the designation אֱלֹהִים *Elōhīm* in all the narratives preceding the revelation of God to Moses on Mount Ḥoreb; a third was P (Priestly Code), which emanated from priestly circles and also refrained from mentioning the name Yhwh before the generation of Moses; there was still a fourth source D, which comprises the main part of the Book of Deuteronomy. It is true that differences of opinion with regard to details were not lacking: one exegete declared this source the earlier and another exegete that source; some attributed a given section or verse to one document and some to another; certain scholars divided a section or verse among the sources in one way and others in another way; there were those who broke down the documents themselves into different strata and others who added new sources to those already mentioned, and so forth.

Nevertheless, even though no two scholars held completely identical views, and though these divergences of opinion betrayed a certain inner weakness in the theory as a whole, yet in regard to the basic principles of the hypothesis almost all the expositors were agreed. Those who opposed the theory, and suggested in its stead different solutions to the problem under discussion, found no support for their proposals; each one of them remained isolated and failed to induce any of the other investigators to forsake the successful view favored by fortune in order to follow him.[2] Possibly this was due to the fact that many of the opponents did not use correct scientific methods, and that even those whose scientific approach was beyond cavil did not succeed in advancing acceptable interpretations of their own. Be this as it may, the documentary hypothesis enjoyed a position of absolute domination in the scientific world. Already in 1924, in the *Zeitschrift für die alttestamentliche Wissenschaft*, the leading periodical for biblical studies in Germany, the editor, H. Gressmann, wrote as follows: "We must stress, with the utmost emphasis, that there is no school of biblical scholarship today that is not founded on the critical analysis of the sources in the Hexateuch, that is, the Pentateuch and the Book of Joshua... and anyone who does not accept the division of the text according to the sources and the results flowing therefrom, has to discharge the onus, if he wishes to be considered a collaborator in our scientific work, of proving that all the research work done till now was futile."

Possibly these words were written just because it was already felt that a new epoch of ferment in biblical criticism was beginning. Even in the circles that had previously been wholly loyal to the documentary hypothesis in all its aspects there arose scholars who commenced to question one or other tenet of the theory and to express misgivings about some of its details. In the very issue in which the editor made the aforementioned statement, W. Staerk, one of the former devotees of the documentary hypothesis, raised certain doubts about the accepted analysis of the sources. In the same year also, M. Löhr published a brochure called *Der Priesterkodex in der Genesis* in which he endeavored to prove, contrary to the prevailing theory to which he, too, had hitherto subscribed, that there is no section or verse in the Book of Genesis that could be attributed to source P. So, too—I am citing, of course, a few examples only—in 1933 P. Volz and W. Rudolph, who were likewise adherents of the documentary theory, wrote a work entitled *Der Elohist als Erzähler: ein Irrweg der Pentateuchkritik?* in which they came to the conclusion that there are no independent narratives in the Pentateuch from source E, but that E, if he existed at all, was at most the redactor of a new and improved edition of source J.

Although the attitude of these savants, in comparison to the exegetical school from which they emanated, appears daring, yet the method of their investigation still resembles the conventional approach, and their contributions are of limited originality. In their view, too, the basis of the doctrine of sources remains firmly established. Even a scholar like Yehezkel Kaufman, who stands outside this school of interpretation and successfully opposes a given portion of its concepts, as he does in his valuable studies on the history of the Israelite religion, still accepts the fundamental principle of the customary division of the text according to sources, and bases his views thereon. Permit me to mention that since 1926 I gave expression to my unqualified opposition to the *entire* doctrine in a series of essays that I published from that year onward, and particularly in a comprehensive work on the Book of Genesis, which appeared in 1934 as one of the publications of the State University of Florence.

As an indication of the spirit prevailing today, it is of interest to mention the fact that in the German periodical referred to above, eleven years after the publication of the astringent remarks of the previous editor against those who refused to accept the documentary hypothesis and its conclusions, there appeared a critique of my aforementioned book from the pen of the new editor, Prof. Hempel, in which he wrote, after some kindly expressions of tribute, which I do not wish to quote here, that in his opinion the treatise "makes an invaluable contribution to the efforts of biblical scholarship to solve the question of the origin of the Book of Genesis." These words clearly show that the possibility of a different solution to the problem from that hitherto accepted by exegetes is recognized even by those who still uphold the conventional interpretation, and stand at the head of the school from which it evolved.

It is worth giving earnest consideration, therefore, to the question of the soundness of the theory that till recently was dominant. To this end it will be necessary, of course, to examine the foundations on which it rests in order to see if, and to what extent, they are strong and valid. I shall undertake this investigation in the succeeding lectures. Today I wish only to make a few prefatory observations concerning the history of the problem and the attempts made to solve it, for even its history may have something to teach us.

I shall not, of course, give a detailed account of the development of the various theories advanced from time to time regarding the origin and composition of the books of the Pentateuch. Doubtless, you are all acquainted with the history of the problem, at least in its main aspects; and, in any event, those who are interested can easily obtain the requisite information from any introductory treatise on the Bible. My purpose is only to indicate briefly the relationship between the course taken by research with respect to our problem and that followed by scholarship relative to the analogous question in Greek literature concerning the works of Homer, to wit, the origin of the two poems, the *Iliad* and *Odyssey*, which are attributed to him. It would be possible, indeed, to compare also the investigations of the epic poetry of the Indians and the studies made of medieval European poetry, but I do not wish to prolong the discussion of the subject unduly. I shall therefore confine myself to some cursory references to matters appertaining to Homer's poems.

The relationship between the history of the Homeric problem and that of the biblical problem has not yet been adequately investigated. But even at this stage, one may state that there is a surprising parallelism between the evolution of views and theories in the two fields of inquiry; in every generation similar concepts and hypotheses prevail at the same time in regard to the Homeric and biblical problems.

In each case, after sporadic doubts had been expressed earlier, systematic criticism began to be voiced in the seventeenth century; the problem was raised in the two branches of study concurrently. In both, the first steps in the development of the exegetical system that was destined to become dominant in the scientific world were taken almost simultaneously. The initial attempt to analyze the sources in the Pentateuch was made by the Protestant priest Witter in a book that was published in Hildesheim in 1711. As

a result of his study of the first chapters of the Book of Genesis,
Witter came to the conclusion that prior to the Torah there existed ancient poetic compositions that served as sources for Moses.
Witter's treatise did not have the good fortune to enjoy wide publicity and was forgotten after a time. However, another book, which
expressed similar views, met with considerable success, namely, the
work of the French physician Astruc, which appeared in Brussels
in 1753 under the title *Conjectures sur les mémoires originaux dont
il paroit que Moyse s'est servi pour composer le livre de la Génèse*.
Astruc was not actually an expert in the subject but only an amateur. Nevertheless this dissertation, in which he examines the whole
Book of Genesis and the beginning of the Book of Exodus and
concludes that Moses made use of two principal documents and
of several fragments belonging to subsidiary sources, has come to
be considered the primary foundation of the new exegesis, and
has gained for Astruc the honor of being called the "father of the
documentary hypothesis." Similarly in the case of Homer's writings, the earliest foundations of the new concepts were laid by
a French dilettante, Abbé d'Aubignac, who was, in consequence,
likewise given the title of "father of the Homeric problem." In
his book *Conjectures académiques ou dissertations sur l'Iliade*, which
was published posthumously in 1715, he, too, expressed the opinion that Homer's poems are not unitary compositions but collec-
tions of poems that were originally wholly unrelated. The works
of Astruc and d'Aubignac resemble each other even in their titles,
both being called *Conjectures*. You may say: Such was the style of
the time and place. True! But this is the very point of interest,
namely, that the mode of the period and country clearly stamped
the labors of the scholars.

The French amateur was followed in each subject by a German
professional scholar who transformed the Frenchman's opinions into
a completely systematized theory: on the one side, Eichhorn, who

published the first edition of his work *Einleitung ins Alte Testament* between the years 1780–83; and on the other, Wolf, whose treatise *Prolegomena ad Homerum* appeared in 1795. In this instance, too, the names of the two works correspond to one another, each being an "Introduction." Also in the present case, the similarity in the names of the books is not a mere coincidence: it is indicative of a like textual approach and similar methods of research. The parallelism of approach and method resulted in analogous conclusions: in regard to the Pentateuch as well as the Homeric poems it was postulated that independent source-documents served as their basis. At first, it is true, the two theories differed in one respect: that insofar as the Torah was concerned, the hypothesis referred to a restricted number of comprehensive documents from each of which were culled various passages that are now integrated in the present pentateuchal books, whereas the Homeric epics were conceived as an amalgam of numerous small, unconnected poems of separate origin. But even this distinction fell away after a while, when, next to the "First Documentary Hypothesis," there arose in biblical exegesis a new thesis called the "Theory of Fragments," which was fully formulated, after a lead had been given in that direction by other scholars, in Vater's commentary to the Book of Genesis, which appeared in the years 1802–5. According to this theory, the Torah was composed of many scrolls that had at first existed independently.

In the early thirties of the nineteenth century, yet another theory, the "Supplement Hypothesis," was advanced in our field of study by Stähelin, Ewald and others. They postulate an ancient basic document, which later generations gradually completed by various additions and through the process of a number of redactions. It was precisely at this time that K.F. Hermann put forward a similar view with reference to Homer in his treatise *De interpolationibus Homeri*, which appeared in 1832. Originally there existed, he held, a basic *Iliad* and *Odyssey,* which were enlarged little by little as a result of various interpolations and a series of recensions.

This doctrine did not endure long in regard to either the Pentateuch or Homer's poems. In his book *Betrachtungen über Homers Ilias* (1837–41), Lachmann validated once more the views concerning the documents from which the epic was composed, and in order to reconstruct these source documents, he developed the analytical method, which was continued and perfected by his successors, until it reached its consummation under Wilamowitz. In like manner, Hupfeld succeeded, a few years after the publication of Lachmann's researches, in renewing and consolidating the documentary hypothesis in the sphere of biblical scholarship, and in founding, on the basis of his late dating of source P and with the help of the analytical method, the "New Documentary Hypothesis," which was amplified by Graf and attained its highest perfection through the labors of Wellhausen, the colleague and friend of Wilamowitz.

It is superfluous to prolong any further our review of the history of this research work in detail. It will suffice to note that the analytical method developed in the two branches of learning on similar lines, particularly the technique of studying repetitions and duplications, contrasts and contradictions, linguistic and stylistic variations and the like, and it led in both fields of investigation to the minutest differentiations and successive dissections, the verses being subjected to microscopic examination. In the end, in biblical as well as Homeric studies, a reaction set in to this exaggerated process of analysis. Possibly the reaction in Greek scholarship is wider and stronger; but it is now being felt in the two spheres together.

What now are we to deduce from this parallelism that continues from one generation to the other? In part, of course, it is to be explained as the result of reciprocal influence, and in part also as due to the general progress in the methods and techniques of research, which is common to all humanistic studies, and in time enables all these branches of learning to develop equally. But undoubtedly it is affected also by the opinions and concepts, the trends and demands, the character and idiosyncrasies of each age. This being so, it may well be that we have before us not an objective discovery of what is actually to be found in the ancient books, but the result of the subjective impression that these writings have on the people of a given environment. If among peoples so different from one another (as I have already indicated, it was possible also to take into account the views of savants concerning the epic poetry of the Indians and of the European nations in the Middle Ages) scholars find literary phenomena so complex and yet so similar, and precisely one trend in one epoch and another trend in another, and yet a third in a third period, the suspicion naturally arises that the investigators' conceptions are not based on purely objective facts but that they were appreciably motivated by the subjective characteristics of the researchers themselves.

Is this scepticism justified? If we wish to find an answer to this question (it is obvious that we may not rely on mere suspicion, until it is truly warranted), we must undertake a new and independent study of the whole problem. We must approach this task with complete objectivity marred by no bias—either towards the views of one school or the opinions of another. We must be prepared, from the outset, to accept the outcome of our inquiry, be it what it may, and feel no anxiety in regard to the honor and sanctity of our Torah. For these transcend literary problems; they belong to the inner content of the books of the Pentateuch and are entirely unaffected by the solution of the literary questions, which concern only their outward form, "the language of men" used by the Torah, to quote the rabbinic dictum. Consequently, it behooves us to conduct our investigation without prejudgment or anticipatory fear, but to rely on the objective examination of the texts themselves and the help afforded by our knowledge of the ancient East, in the cultural environment of which the children of Israel lived when the Torah was written. Let us not approach the scriptural passages with the literary and aesthetic criteria of our time, but let us apply to them the standards obtaining in the ancient East generally and among the people of Israel particularly.

I have engaged in these researches many years, and I have given the results of my work in a bulky volume, which I ventured to mention to you a little while ago. But I wrote this book in a language that is known to but a limited number among you. I have therefore decided to talk to you, during this course, on the contents of this treatise and on my studies subsequent to its publication—in outline only, of course. I invite you to retrace with me the course of my work, to examine with me the material that I examined, to study with me the subjects I studied, to attempt, along with me, to draw such conclusions from this examination and study as shall appear to us to be the most justified and correct. I invite you, in fact, to enter with me that beautiful and majestic edifice of the documentary hypothesis, which was erected and completed by the devoted and industrious labor of many generations of distinguished workers, that mighty structure in which European scholarship has hitherto taken so much pride—to enter it with me and to test, together with me, its soundness and the stability of the pillars upon which it rests. All honor is due to those who built it and brought it to completion; we must not belittle them or their labors, from which we can undoubtedly learn a great deal. Yet we have the right to probe them and to test the materials out of which they were built and the method of their structure. Since we are nearer than they to the spirit of the Bible, and our knowledge of the ancient East is more extensive and exact today than it was at the time when their edifice was erected, we may perchance see something that escaped their attention, or solve some riddle to which they strove in vain to find a solution.

The documentary hypothesis is founded mainly on the *narrative* portions of the Pentateuch, and especially on the Book of Genesis. It follows therefore that we, too, must make Genesis and the problems connected with it the focal point of our study. We shall not deal with the questions relating to the Torah *statutes*, which form a separate subject, or with the problems pertaining to the Book of Deuteronomy, which also require special investigation on their own.[3] If in the end we find that the dominant view concerning Genesis is right, then we must conclude that the documentary theory is well-founded, and if not—then its negation in regard to Genesis implies the refutation of the entire hypothesis.

The arguments in favor of the differentiation of various documents in the Book of Genesis, which constitute, as we have explained, the pillars supporting the entire structure of the documentary theory, are five, to wit:

(a) the use of different names for the Deity;
(b) variations of language and style;
(c) contradictions and divergences of view;
(d) duplications and repetitions;
(e) signs of composite structure in the sections.

These five pillars we shall examine in the coming lectures. We shall see if they rest on a firm foundation, if they are hewn from hard rock, and if they are strong enough to bear the weight of the structure. As a result of our investigation, we shall be able to decide whether the building can still be considered solid and sound, or whether, on the contrary, it is something that is irretrievably doomed.

THE DIVINE NAMES

AS I STATED YESTERDAY, the structure of the theory hitherto dominant in biblical scholarship rests on five pillars. This is the theory known as the "Documentary Hypothesis," which postulates that the Pentateuch was composed by the amalgamation of sections and subsections derived from four independent source-documents, J, E, P, D. Our task is to make closer acquaintance with these pillars and to examine them, in order to see whether they are strong and durable, as most scholars think, or not. We shall begin this investigation today. We shall enter the building, approach the pillars, and subject them and the material of which they are made to detailed and exact scrutiny. We shall together recapitulate the work that I have done in recent years, and which I described in my Italian treatise on the Book of Genesis. I shall be very happy to act as your guide on this tour.

Manifestly it will not be possible, in the course of a few lectures, to review the whole subject fully in all its varied aspects. Nevertheless, if we shall succeed in reviewing the principal arguments and some of the most important illustrative texts, it will, I believe, suffice for the time being. Those who desire to study the

matter further can refer to my aforementioned book (if the language does not prove an obstacle), where they will find the details
that lack of time prevents me from mentioning here.

Let us begin with the first pillar, the use of different names
for God.[1] The fact that the divine names vary in the Pentateuch,
that is, that sometimes we find there the name 'ה YHWH [ren-
dered, on the basis of its traditional pronunciation *Adhōnay*, by
"Lord"] and sometimes אֱלֹהִים *Elōhīm* ["God"] (apart from other
names that occur only occasionally, like אֵל *El* ["God"], אֵל עֶלְיוֹן
El 'Elyōn ["God Most High"], שַׁדַּי *Šadday* ["Almighty"], אֵל שַׁדַּי *El
Šadday* ["God Almighty"], and the like), served as the starting
point of the studies of Witter and Astruc and their successors;
and in the course of generations it constituted the main evidence
adduced in support of the documentary hypothesis. Latterly, after
biblical research had become greatly enlarged and ramified in accordance with the analytical method, which had been perfected
in every aspect and detail, this argument lost some of its earlier
importance, and sometimes is no longer counted as one of the
theory's chief proofs. Yet the fact remains that it is precisely on the
results of the study of the variant use of the divine names that the
other arguments were primarily based. On the other hand, even
those exegetes who do not give primacy today to the argument
of the names refrain from doing so not because they consider
the matter unimportant, but because, in the course of time, the
question of the divine names has become something that is self-
understood and no longer needs special emphasis. It follows, therefore, that this is in truth the ultimate foundation of the documentary hypothesis, not only historically but also theoretically. Hence
we must deal with it first.

The nature of the difficulty is quite clear. We find, for example, in the first section of Genesis: *In the beginning* 'Elōhīm *created the heavens and the earth. As for the earth... but the spirit of*
'Elōhīm *was hovering over the face of the waters. And* 'Elōhīm *said,*

'Let there be light'; and there was light, and so on. No other divine name, save *'Elōhīm,* occurs until the end of the first narrative
concerning the Creation, that is, till the words *which* 'Elōhīm *had
creatively made* (ii 3). Immediately thereafter we read: *This is the
history of the heavens and the earth when they were created, in the
day that* YHWH 'Elōhīm *made the earth and the heavens* (ii 4), and
so forth, YHWH *'Elōhīm* being almost always used till the end of
the story of the Garden of Eden, that is, to the end of chapter
iii. I said *almost* always because three times, in this section, the
name *'Elōhīm* occurs alone (iii 1, 3, 5). Later, at the beginning of
chapter iv, it is written: *I have created a man equally with* YHWH;
the name YHWH also occurs several times more in this section,
but at the end (iv 25) we read: *For 'Elōhīm has appointed for me
another child.* So, too, in the subsequent passages, the names keep
changing. In the story of the Flood, we sometimes find YHWH and
sometimes *'Elōhīm.* In the section of the Covenant of the Pieces
(ch. xv) YHWH occurs, and in that of the Circumcision (xvii 3f.)
we find *'Elōhīm.* There is no need to cite any further examples.

Naturally, the question occurs to the reader: why this change
of names? The answer of the documentary hypothesis is known.
There are sections here emanating from different sources: one document, source J, used the name YHWH; a second document, E,
employed the name *'Elōhīm;* a third document, P, also made use
of the name *'Elōhīm* (while source D does not appear at all in
the Book of Genesis). At a given stage, a redactor came and took
some sections from this source, some portions from that source,
and some extracts from the third document. He placed them in
juxtaposition, or fused them together, but left to each one its initial form and even the divine names originally found therein. In
this way, the present composite book acquired the different designations for God with which we are now confronted. It is just
this variation of names, as we have stated, that gave rise to the

conjecture that the Torah was pieced together from these documents, and this concept became the central pillar of the documentary hypothesis. There was, to be sure, no lack of other attempts to solve the problem in various ways, but these were either not very satisfactory or failed to offer a complete explanation of the facts; in any event, they remained experimental and were not widely accepted among scholars. Not one of them succeeded in shaking for a moment the main foundation of the dominant view, and there is no need therefore to detail them here.

Similarly, it would be superfluous to raise objections of a general nature against the solution proposed by the documentary hypothesis. If we wish our investigation to result in trustworthy conclusions, we cannot be content with a general review, but we must thoroughly probe the details of the theory, re-examining the origin of the problem from its earliest inception, and endeavoring, in particular, to penetrate to the innermost meaning of the biblical passages and to draw from the texts themselves the answers to our questions. Let us consult the book; let us listen to the verses and hear what they tell us.

One thing appears to me to be beyond doubt, namely, that the variations in the choice of the divine names did not come about accidentally but by design. The view has, indeed, recently been expressed that the two designations, YHWH and *'Elōhīm*, are absolutely identical in meaning, and are interchanged according to the wish of the writer for subjective reasons that the reader cannot comprehend.[2] But it is difficult to concur in this opinion. Surely the Torah, whose primary aim is to guide man towards the knowledge of the Lord and the keeping of His way, did not use the Lord's names indiscriminately, like some careless scribe who writes as the passing whim dictates. The language of the Torah is always scrupulously exact in its minutest details, and it is inconceivable that just in this respect, the most important and exalted, it failed to act with meticulous care and exactitude. We must conclude, therefore, that there is, without doubt, some significance in the changing of the names. What is it?

Before we undertake to solve this problem, we must first consider the character of the two names. They are not of the same type. The designation *Elōhīm* was originally a common noun, an appellative, that was applied both to the One God of Israel and to the heathen gods (as was the name *'El*). On the other hand, the name Yhwh is a proper noun, the specific name of Israel's God, the God whom the Israelites acknowledged as the Sovereign of the universe and as the Divinity who chose them as His people. Let me cite a parallel by way of illustration. A certain city may be called *Jerusalem* or simply *city*. The appellation *city* is common to her and to all other cities; the name *Jerusalem* belongs to her alone. When the ancestors of the Jewish people realized that there is but One God, and that only "Yhwh, He is *Elōhīm*" (i Kings xviii 39), then the common substantive *Elōhīm* also acquired for them the signification of a proper noun, and became synonymous with the name Yhwh. If Jerusalem had been the sole city in the world of those who spoke Hebrew, then of course the word *city* would have become a proper name, synonymous with *Jerusalem*. This was actually the case in the past, at the time when Jerusalem was the one important city in the country. But as a rule synonyms are not quite identical in meaning, and this is true in the present instance, too. The original connotation of the name *Elōhīm*, its use as an appellative, could not be completely forgotten. It was impossible for one who spoke or wrote Hebrew not to be aware that only the name Yhwh expressed the particular personality of Israel's God; and on the other hand, he could not fail to be conscious of the fact that the deities of the gentiles were also designated *Elōhīm*, and that only when all the nations would recognize, as did Israel, that "Yhwh, *He is Elōhīm*," "would Yhwh be One and *His name One*" (Zechariah xiv 9).

The same applies to Judah's capital: at the very time when the people called it just *city* they could not be unmindful, on the one hand, that there were nevertheless other cities in the world, and, on the other, that only the name *Jerusalem* was capable of arousing in the soul of the reader or listener all those memories, sentiments and yearnings that history has forever associated with this name and this name only.

Having grasped this principle, let us proceed further. Let us investigate the way in which the two divine names are used, and see if we can possibly explain their usage on the basis of the rule that we have just formulated. Obviously, in order to gain full understanding of the significance underlying the use of the two names in the Pentateuch, it is desirable that we should also study the manner in which they are employed in the other books of the Bible—in the Prophets and the Hagiographa. It is also manifest that, for the purpose of this inquiry, we must confine ourselves to the instances where *'Elōhīm* is used strictly in the capacity of a proper noun, as a synonym of YHWH, and as a substitute for it. We shall take no account of it, therefore, in the following cases:

(a) When it is used as a simple appellative, e.g., ii Kings i 3, 6, 16: *Is it because there is no* GOD [*'Elōhīm*] *in Israel...?*;

(b) when it refers to the pagan deities, for instance, in the well-known phrase *other* GODS [*'Elōhīm*], or to some divine entity, as in Hosea xii 4: *and by his strength he strove with a* GODLIKE *being* [*'Elōhīm*];

(c) when it occurs in the construct, for example, in expressions like *the* GOD OF [*'Elōhē*] *Israel, the* GOD OF [*'Elōhē*] *our fathers*, and the like;

(d) when it has a possessive suffix—*your* GOD [*'Elōhekhā*], *our* GOD [*'Elōhēnū*], and so forth;

(e) when it occurs in stereotyped composite phrases, like *man of* GOD [*'Elohīm*], *visions of* GOD [*'Elōhīm*], *wrestlings of* GOD [*'Elōhīm*; E.V. "mighty wrestlings"], and similar expressions, which are intended only to indicate the divine nature of the subject referred to, as though one were to say: *a godly man, divine visions, godlike wrestlings.*

To sum up: the name *'Elōhīm* will come under consideration only in those instances in which it might have been possible to substitute the Tetragrammaton, without any other alteration of the form of the sentence. A case in point is the opening verse of the Book of Genesis: *In the beginning* 'Elōhīm *created the heavens and the earth,* for it was possible to write instead: In the beginning YHWH created the heavens and the earth.

Following this rule, let us now examine the position in each of the various categories of biblical literature. We shall begin with the Prophets.

In the *prophetic* writings, the name *'Elōhīm* is never used at all in place of YHWH. The name of Israel's God in the books of the Prophets is always and only YHWH. An exception is provided by the Book of Jonah, where *'Elōhīm* occurs a number of times as the proper name of the God of Israel, but this is an exception that proves the rule; for although Jonah is included in the section of the Prophets in the classification of the biblical books, it belongs, from the viewpoint of its content, not to the prophetic but to the narrative literature. Another exception to this rule we find in the second part of the Book of Isaiah, which frequently uses, in place of the Tetragrammaton, a word that was originally a common noun—not, indeed, the name *'Elōhīm* but *'El.* But of this I shall speak in tomorrow's lecture.

In the *legal* literature, that is, in all the sections of the Pentateuch and of Ezekiel appertaining to the precepts, only YHWH occurs as the personal name of God.

The *poetic* writings, with the exception of such poems as belong to the category of wisdom literature or have been influenced by it (like those I am about to mention now), also have no proper name for God other than the Tetragrammaton.

In the wisdom literature, the position is altogether different. In the poetic portion of the Book of Job the name YHWH does not occur except once (xii 9); but the text in this passage is uncertain, for a number of manuscripts read *'Elōhīm* instead. This verse apart, there occur regularly in place of the Tetragrammaton names that were originally appellatives, to wit, *'El, 'Elōah, 'Elōhīm,* or the name *Šadday*. In the Book of Ecclesiastes, the divine name is invariably *'Elōhīm*, and the name YHWH is not mentioned even once. Likewise in the Book of Proverbs, the names *'Elōhīm* and *'Elōah* are sometimes found. Ecclesiasticus also frequently uses the names *'El* and *'Elōhīm*. In a number of psalms, especially in the Second and Third Books (the Elohistic books), the names *'El* and *'Elōhīm* enjoy primacy. In this connection, we should bear in mind that many psalms show the influence of the wisdom literature, and some of them unquestionably belong to it. Similarly, the names *'El* and *'Elōhīm* are found in *the last words of David* (ii Sam. xxiii 1-7), which are undoubtedly connected with the sapiential literature.

In the *narrative* literature, that is, in the narrative sections of the Pentateuch, the Earlier Prophets (Joshua to ii Kings), the Book of Jonah, the narrative portion of Job, and so forth, the Tetragrammaton and *'Elōhīm* are both used—in close proximity.

These are the facts. Having noted that the *wisdom* literature differs, relative to our subject, from all the other forms of literature, and seeing that the sapiential category is a universal type of writing and that many of its characteristics are shared by compositions of this class among all the diverse peoples of the ancient East, we must make a study of the wisdom literature of the other nations, too. It is true that the ethos of Israel succeeded in leaving its impress also on the wisdom books of our people; nevertheless they approximate in many respects the sapiential works produced outside the Israelite ranks. It will not be superfluous, therefore, to take a glance at the surrounding domains.

But as soon as we begin to study them, we are struck by an amazing phenomenon. The wisdom books of the ancient East, irrespective of the people from which they emanated or the language in which they were written, usually refer to the Godhead by an appellative rather than by the *proper* names of the various divinities.

In the sapiential writings of the Egyptians the term mostly used is the common noun *nṯr*, corresponding to *'Elōah* or *'Elōhīm* in Hebrew. This practice we already find in the most ancient texts, like those that have reached us in the Papyrus Prisse (ii 2: "The ways of the god are not known"), or the Instruction for King Meri-ka-Re (61 and 130: "The god knows all the names"). So it continued for hundreds of years, until the period of the efflorescence of Hebrew literature: for example, in the Proverbs of Amen-em-Opet (18: "The god in his perfection and man in his imperfection"), or in the Proverbs of Ani (35: "The god—to him belongs the revelation of truth"). The names of the different deities appear only occasionally, particularly in two circumstances: a) when the writer quotes traditional sayings that have been handed down in a fixed form, for instance: "The help of Re (the sun-god) is from afar" (Proverbs of Amen-em-Opet, 26); b) when he alludes to the distinctive attributes of a given god, for example: "Despise not one who is older than you; he saw Re before you" (27).

Similarly, the Babylonians were accustomed to use the appellative *ilu*, that is, *'ēl* ("god"). We read, for instance, in the book called today the Babylonian Ecclesiastes: "In place of riches *ilu* brought poverty" (75); "Since you seek not the counsel of *ilu*, what shall your fate be?" (217). But the Babylonian sages also employ proper names whenever there is a particular occasion for this. We

find, for example, in the aforementioned book (235) the phrase
"The work of the hands of Aruru" as an expression for man, for
according to the accepted tradition of the Babylonians, it is specifically the goddess Aruru who created man.

This is also the case in the Aramaic version of the Romance
of Aḥiqar. The word אֱלָהִין *Elāhīn* or אֱלָהַיָּא *Elāhayyā* in the plural
occurs there several times, and although most scholars regard it as
a numerical plural, and explain it to mean *gods* or *the gods*, it is a
fact that at least once (col. viii, 1. 115) the verb connected with
it is in the singular, as is customary in Hebrew in relation to the
name *Elōhīm*. The reading should not, of course, be corrected to
אֱלָהָא *Elāhā* in the singular, as some scholars have suggested; it
seems more probable that here, and in other passages, the plural
has a singular sense, exactly as in the case of *Elōhīm*. This view is
supported by the fact that in the Letter of Ḥananiah, which was
discovered in the same collection of papyri to which the fragments
of the Aramaic recension of the Romance of Aḥiqar belong, the
plural *Elāhayyā* occurs again, and there it is extremely difficult
to regard it as a numerical plural, since the author is one of the
pious Jews of the Land of Israel. It is thus seen that we also find
in the wisdom literature written in Aramaic the same peculiarity
that we observed in Egyptian and Akkadian writings. In Aramaic,
too, the proper names of the deities appear only occasionally, here
and there (for example, *Šamaš, ibid.,* col. vi, 11. 92, 93).

In fine: in all branches of the wisdom literature, the gentile
peoples are accustomed to use general names for the Godhead
rather than the proper names of the various divinities. To determine
the underlying significance of this is a difficult and complicated
matter with which we cannot deal now. Possibly the international
character of the sapiential writings was one of the factors responsible for this usage, causing the general idea of the Deity, which is
common to all peoples, to be preferred to the particular concepts
of the divinities specific to the individual nations. In any case, the

solution to this problem is not important for our subject; it suffices that we have determined the facts as we saw them.

Now, on the basis of what we have observed thus far, let us endeavor to clarify the position in the different categories of Hebrew literature.

In those categories that have a purely Israelite character, only the Tetragrammaton occurs, this being the national name of God, expressing the personal conception of the Deity exclusive to Israel. The national character of biblical prophecy, the resolute opposition of the prophets to all currents of thought emanating from the neighboring peoples, and above all their complete realization that they were the mouthpiece of the God of Israel Himself, and not of some abstract, indeterminate divinity, conduced to the fact that, in the prophetic literature, YHWH, Israel's traditional name for the Deity, which referred specifically to the God of Israel, was used exclusively. Only the Second Isaiah, who was influenced to a certain extent by the Psalms, which, in turn, are related to the wisdom literature, sometimes employs 'El as a proper name. But, as I have indicated, I shall speak of the special factors responsible for this characteristic on another occasion.

The explanation of the usage in the prophetic writings applies also to the legal literature. The latter mentions only the Tetragrammaton, because the source of the statutes and ordinances is the actual will of YHWH, who has chosen His people and has given them His Torah.

The same position obtains in biblical *poetry*, which is the direct and spontaneous expression of the soul of the people, who are accustomed to think of their God in personal terms. The extent to which the practice prevailed among the general population of using the Tetragrammaton in daily life we now know from the Lachish texts. When the writer greets his friend, he uses the Divine Name ("May YHWH cause my lord to hear tidings of peace," and so on); when he takes an oath, he swears by the Name, and even apart from these conventional expressions, he mentions the Tetragrammaton only. The name *Elōhīm* is not found once in all the Lachish Letters. This is paralleled by the greetings recorded in the Bible (Judges vi 12; Psalms cxxix 8; Ruth ii 4), to which I shall revert subsequently. I shall likewise explain later on how this premise enables us to understand the rabbinic enactment that a man should use the Name in greeting his fellow.

On the other hand, our *wisdom* literature has been influenced appreciably by the tradition of the general sapiential writings, of which I have already spoken. The teachers of wisdom in Israel identified the non-specific *'El* of the gentile sages with their One God, and following the literary practice of the wise men of other nations, they, too, frequently employed the generic terms *'El*, *'Elōah*, *'Elōhīm*, preferring them to the national name, YHWH. Only Proverbs forms an exception; possibly its compilers wished to give to the universal material of the book an Israelitish quality also in this respect, that *mainly* they used the national name for God— mainly, but not invariably. In the Psalms, which often show the influence of the wisdom literature, the use of general names for the Deity, like *'El* and *'Elōhīm*, instead of the Tetragrammaton, is not infrequently due to reasons similar to those mentioned above. The prevailing view that in the Elohistic Psalms the name *'Elōhīm* is not original, and that only in a later period did the scribes substitute it for the Tetragrammaton, which was written there in the first instance, is only partly correct. Although it may be conjectured that such was the case in some psalms, in certain other psalms *'Elōhīm* was undoubtedly fully intended by the author. When the poet wished to convey the general idea of divinity, or to mention the Almighty as the God of the whole world, as the Creator of the entire universe, as the Deity of all peoples, he gave preference to the general names. This tendency is clearly seen in several psalms: thus, for instance, Psalm xlvii, which is a song of praise to the Almighty as the God of the whole earth, opens with the words: *Clap your hands, all peoples! Shout to* ʾElōhīm *with loud songs of joy!* "All nations," even those who know not Yʜwʜ (if they knew Him, they would already be part of Israel), recognize at least *ʾElōhīm*, the universal conception of the Godhead; hence the poet invites them to clap their hands and to shout specifically to *ʾElōhīm*. Thereafter he continues: *For* Yʜwʜ, *the Most High, is terrible, a great king over all the earth.* His intention is to tell us that Yʜwʜ, the God acknowledged and worshipped by the children of Israel, reigns not only over Israel, but over the whole earth. In the continuation of the psalm we are told: *ʾElōhīm has gone up with a shout,* Yʜwʜ *with the sound of a trumpet*; the two names are parallel to each other in the two lines, because, as we have stated, they are identical, Yʜwʜ being *ʾElōhīm*. The same obtains in Psalm lxviii, and in many other psalms. The position is similar, to a certain extent, to what we found in the wisdom literature of the other peoples, who use a general term when they wish to convey the general concept of Deity, and proper names when they desire to refer to the distinctive character and attributes of their gods. I said "similar to a certain extent," since there is actually a vast difference between the two. The resemblance lies in the literary form; the divergence is conceptual. The great innovation on the part of the Israelites consists in the fact that, while the writings of the pagans give expression, on the one hand, to the abstract and general notion of divinity, and, on the other, make mention of some particular god, in Hebrew literature the concept of the specific God of Israel is completely identified with that of the God of the whole earth. Yʜwʜ, whom the children of Israel recognize and before whom they prostrate themselves, is none other than *ʾElōhīm*, of whose dominion over them all men are more or less clearly conscious, and whom they are destined to acknowledge fully in time to come. This is the sublime thought to which the biblical poets give expression through the variation of the names.

Since, however, the practice developed to mention ʾ*Elōhīm* and ʾ*El* for a specific reason, and thus these names became a common stylistic feature of the Psalms, the poets were led to employ them even without special intention. This explains the occurrence of such names even in psalms that show no trace of having been directly influenced by the wisdom literature, or any desire to give particular emphasis to the general idea of the Godhead.

One other observation has to be made with regard to the Book of Psalms. Although, as I have stated a little while ago, we cannot accept the view that *all* the Elohistic psalms originally contained the Tetragrammaton and that only in a later redaction was ʾ*Elōhīm* substituted for it by the scribes, yet in the case of a number of these psalms, we must postulate that such a change was actually made; a comparison of Psalm liii with Psalm xiv, and expressions like אֱלֹהִים אֱלֹהֵינוּ ʾ*Elōhīm* ʾ*Elōhēnū* provide clear evidence of this. However, the change of name was not brought about for the reason customarily supposed, that is, in order to avoid using the Tetragrammaton for reasons of piety. Were this the purpose of the scribes, they would simply have made ʾ*Elōhīm* the *q*ᵉ*rē* [the word to be read] for the *keth*ī*bh* [the word that is written] Yʜᴡʜ, as in fact it has become traditional to read ʾ*Adhōnay* in place of the latter; but they would not have ventured to tamper with the text and alter it. The very opposite tendency is to be discerned here—the tendency to give precedence to the name ʾ*Elōhīm* over the Tetragrammaton. Certain circles that came under the influence of cosmopolitan currents of thought apparently considered that the avoidance of the proper name of the Deity and the preference given to the generic name were indicative of progress and a higher religious outlook; in these coteries not only were new Elohistic psalms composed, but some of the old psalms were "amended" in harmony with this trend.

What now of the narrative literature, which uses both Yʜᴡʜ and ʾ*Elōhīm*? I propose to discuss this subject in my next lecture.

MORE ABOUT THE DIVINE NAMES

WE SPOKE YESTERDAY of the manner in which the various divine names—on the one side the Tetragrammaton, and on the other, the name *'Elōhīm* and those akin to it, like *'Elōah* or *'El*—are used throughout the Scriptures, and we found that in all branches of Hebrew literature having a purely Israelite content—for example, the prophetic writings, the legal sections, and the poetic literature insofar as it has a national or folk character—the personal name of God is always YHWH, and the other names serve only as appellatives. Conversely, in the wisdom literature and in the poetry that has been more or less influenced by it, whose subject matter is not exclusive to Israel but is of universal import (for instance, the poetic section of Job, the Book of Ecclesiastes and the like; and so, too, those psalms whose aim is to praise the Lord not only as the God of Israel but as the God of humanity, and to invite all mankind to join Israel in acknowledging and serving Him), the most usual name is *'Elōhīm* or some other designation that was likewise to begin with an appellative, such as *'Elōah* or *'El*. We have also seen that this difference in the choice of the divine names flows on the one hand from the original meaning of the names and on the other from the literary tradition of the ancient East.

Now we must turn to the *narrative* literature, which holds, in regard to the divine names, an intermediate position between the categories of literature that employ only the Tetragrammaton and those that prefer *'Elōhīm* and cognate appellations.

But before we deal with the subject proper, we must make another preliminary observation, to wit, that the difference we established in the principles governing the use of the divine names continued also in the post-biblical period, up to our own times; this shows how deep its roots are in the usage of the language, in its literary tradition, and in the national ethos. It is manifestly impossible, in the short time at our disposal, to cover all the details relevant to the employment of the divine names in every period of Jewish history; but we can indicate a few of the important points, which will suffice to clarify the subject in general.

Point one: the conflict between the Sadducees and the Pharisees. We know that the Pharisaic sages enacted that a man should mention the Name in greeting his fellow; I alluded to this yesterday. Divergent opinions have been expressed in regard to the time, the causes and the purpose of this enactment; but it seems to me that the correct way to understand it is to connect it with the attitude of the various Jewish parties in Israel towards the different names for God.

The *Minim* ("Sectarians"), that is, the Sadducees, being members of the aristocracy, were influenced by the international wisdom of the time, and especially by Greek thought, which was also accustomed, like the ancient universal wisdom, to designate the Godhead by his general name. They were inclined to regard this attitude as progressive vis-à-vis the national tradition, which clung to the proper name YHWH, and they preferred to use generic appellations. This is not a groundless conjecture: we find, in point of fact, that the Book of the Covenant of the Damascus

Community, published by Solomon Schechter* (be the group from which it emanated what it may, its theology nevertheless approximates that of the Sadduceans), always refers to God as 'El. Even when it quotes a biblical verse that in the original contained the Tetragrammaton, it changes the reading and substitutes 'El for YHWH, in exactly the same way as in previous generations the scribes had "amended" the ancient psalms and introduced 'Elōhīm in place of the name YHWH used by the author. But the Pharisees, who belonged to the lower classes, and supported their national outlook, and were meticulous in preserving the national form of the faith, were opposed to this doctrine, which was detrimental to the national tradition and liable to weaken in the heart of the people the sense of direct contact with YHWH, their God. Hence they ordained that, on the contrary, even in secular affairs, even in the salutation between a man and his fellow, the Tetragrammaton should be employed. This was not, in truth, an innovation on the part of the (Pharisaic) Sages, for we have already seen from the Lachish Letters and the formulas of greeting mentioned in the Bible that this was the folk custom since earliest times; however, the Rabbis wished formally to proclaim their approval and confirmation of this custom, in opposition to the teaching of the "Sectaries."

The second point is related to the first: In Talmudic and Midrashic literature you find numerous names and designations for God, such as *the Holy One blessed be He, Master of the universe, our Father in heaven, the Omnipresent* and many similar terms. But you do not find 'El, or 'Elōah, or 'Elōhīm used as proper names synonymous with the Tetragrammaton. There are, it is true, idiomatic expressions like 'Elōhē Yiśrā'ēl ["the God of Israel"], and likewise forms declined with the personal suffixes ('Elōhekhā ["your

---

* Under the title *Documents of Jewish Sectaries, Fragments of a Zadokite Work*, 2 vols. Cambridge, 1910.

God" (mas. sing.)], *'Elōhāw* ["his God"], etc.); but in these instances, where they occur in the construct or with the addition
of the possessive suffixes, they are, of course, purely common
nouns. So, too, the phrase *'Elōhīm ḥayyīm* is just a general term,
signifying: "the living God." The *single* words *'El, 'Elōah, 'Elōhīm*,
which occur in the Bible, are completely wanting in Talmudic
literature in relation to the God of Israel, as though the Rabbis
wished, for the reason stated, to abolish their use in lieu of the
Tetragrammaton. They are employed only to signify the heathen
gods or the Deity in general; in reference to the One God—and
this is an exception that proves the rule—they are found solely
in conversations with gentiles.

As for the Aramaic translations of the Bible, which are prod-
ucts of the rabbinic schools, it is characteristic that in the Targum
of Onkelos we find invariably, and in the other Targumim mostly,
the Tetragrammaton (written יְ"י YY), even in those passages in
which the original has *'Elōhīm*. So, too, in the liturgy, which likewise emanates from the rabbinic academies, the proper name is
always YHWH (pronounced, of course, *'Adhōnay*), whilst the name
'Elōhīm and similar designations occur purely as common nouns,
used in the construct or with the addition of possessive suffixes
or with adjectives.

Another point: The word *'Elōhīm* begins to appear once more as
a proper name in the philosophical literature of the Middle Ages,
that is, in the writings of the scholars who come under the influence of the international culture of the day, when these savants
desire to use a term befitting the philosophic conception of God.
Similar circumstances to those prevailing in ancient times thus
brought about similar results. Also in modern Hebrew, insofar as we
are exact in our choice of words, we employ the Tetragrammaton
when we have in mind the traditional Jewish idea of the Deity,
and the name *'Elōhīm* when we wish to express the philosophic
or universal concept of the Godhead.

It follows from all this that the existence of the basic difference referred to between the name Yʜwʜ on the one hand, and *ʾElōhīm* and cognate appellations on the other, is not to be doubted. Starting from this premise, we may now approach the principal problem itself, the question of the use of the divine names in the narrative literature, and especially in the narrative sections of the Torah.

First of all, we must note that the subject matter of the narrative literature is not entirely of a national Israelite character. It embodies the general traditional material of the ancient East, elements that are derived from the sources of the wisdom literature or have passed through its channels, and it contains tales of world events, in which Israelite and gentile memories are interwoven and fused. This enables us to draw the first conclusion: the fact that the narrative writings occupy, in regard to the use of the Sacred names, an intermediate position between the national categories of literature, which employ only the Tetragrammaton, and the wisdom literature, which prefers the names that were originally common substantives, can in general be satisfactorily explained by the composite character of its contents, which include some features that are close to the former literary types and others that approximate the latter class.

But this is not enough. We must go further and endeavor, especially in connection with the Pentateuch, which is our immediate task, to elucidate the position fully, not only in its general aspect but also in detail. In other words, we must clarify, to the best of our ability, why just in certain sections or verses the Torah narratives have the Tetragrammaton and in others *ʾElōhīm*. Is it possible to formulate rules with regard to the use of the names in proximity to each other? I believe that we are able to answer this question affirmatively. On the basis of what we have stated so far, we may assume that in each case the Torah chose one of

the two names according to the context and intention, precisely
as follows:

It selected the name YHWH when the text reflects the Israelite
conception of God, which is embodied in the portrayal of YHWH
and finds expression in the attributes traditionally ascribed to Him
by Israel, particularly in His ethical character; it preferred the name
'Elōhīm when the passage implies the abstract idea of the Deity
prevalent in the international circles of "wise men"—God conceived
as the Creator of the physical universe, as the Ruler of nature, as
the Source of life.

The Tetragrammaton is used when expression is given to the
direct, intuitive notion of God, which characterizes the simple faith
of the multitude or the ardor of the prophetic spirit; the name
'Elōhīm, when the concept of thinkers who meditate on the lofty
problems connected with the existence of the world and humanity is to be conveyed.

The name YHWH occurs when the context depicts the divine
attributes in relatively lucid and, as it were, palpable terms, a clear
picture being conveyed; 'Elōhīm, when the portrayal is more general, superficial and hazy, leaving an impression of obscurity.

The Tetragrammaton is found when the Torah seeks to arouse
in the soul of the reader or the listener the feeling of the sublim-
ity of the Divine Presence in all its majesty and glory; the name
'Elōhīm, when it wishes to mention God in an ordinary manner,
or when the expression or thought may not, out of reverence, be
associated directly with the Holiest Name.

The name YHWH is employed when God is presented to us in
His personal character and in direct relationship to people or nature;
and 'Elōhīm, when the Deity is alluded to as a Transcendental Being
who exists completely outside and above the physical universe.

The Tetragrammaton appears when the reference is to the God
of Israel relative to His people or to their ancestors; 'Elōhīm, when

He is spoken of in relation to one who is not a member of the Chosen People.

Yhwh is mentioned when the theme concerns Israel's tradition; and *'Elōhīm*, when the subject matter appertains to the universal tradition.

Sometimes, of course, it happens that two opposite rules apply together and come in conflict with each other; then, as logic demands, the rule that is more material to the primary purport of the relevant passage prevails.

Let us now see if, and to what extent, the texts conform to these rules that resulted from our investigation. If they do, this conformity serves as corroborative proof of the correctness of our conclusions, and will permit us to elucidate—and this is most important—the reasons underlying the change of names.

It is self-understood that in the course of this lecture it will not be possible for us to examine all the pentateuchal narratives, or even the Book of Genesis in its entirety; consequently, we shall have to content ourselves with selections. However, in order that we may obtain decisive proof, we shall not choose our passages sporadically, but we shall commence our examination at the beginning of Genesis, and we shall follow the order of the text without any omissions until we feel that we have sufficient material on which to base sound conclusions.

In the story of Creation, God appears as the Creator of the physical universe and as the Lord of the world, who has dominion over everything. All that exists was formed by His fiat alone, without direct contact between Him and nature. Hence, according to our rules, the Bible should use here the name *'Elōhīm*; in point of fact, only *'Elōhīm* occurs throughout the section. Possibly an added reason for the use of the name *'Elōhīm* is to be found in the fact that the description of the work of creation is connected, in many respects, with the general tradition of the ancient East and the cosmopolitan ideas that reached Israel through the wisdom literature. Conceivably one may object at this stage: but the last paragraph of the section speaks of the Sabbath, which is a precept exclusive to Israel, and therefore the Israelite name of God was required. To this one may reply that, on the contrary, it was the specific intention of the Torah here to teach us that the sanctity of the Sabbath flows from cosmic reasons, and antedates Israel, and rests on the world as a whole. Although the commandments appertaining to the manner of observing the Sabbath, which were subsequently prescribed in the Torah, are incumbent only on Israel, yet the Sabbath *per se* was hallowed from the time that the world came into being, and its sanctity is not something restricted to the people of Israel. Confirmation of this view is to be seen in the fact that at the revelation at Mount Sinai Israel was told: *Remember the Sabbath day, to keep it holy*, but not: *know* that there is a Sabbath in the world; that was already common knowledge. Possibly Scripture discerns a dim recollection of the holiness of the Sabbath in the day *Šapattu* or *Šabattu* of the Babylonians, and the holiness that they and many other peoples ascribed to the number seven.

In the story of the Garden of Eden, on the other hand, God is portrayed as the moral Ruler, for He imposes a certain injunction on man, symbolic of the ritual precepts that are subsequently to be given to Israel, and He requires an accounting from him for his actions. This apart, emphasis is laid here on His personal aspect, exemplified in His direct relations with man and the other creatures. For these reasons, the Tetragrammaton was required here; and this is precisely what we find (only in the words of the serpent, who represents the principle of evil, and in the speech of the woman when she converses with him, is this name, out of reverence, not used). Although some details of the story show a certain connection with non-Israelite traditions, these are but details; the heart of the narrative is its moral content, and it is this that decides the choice of the divine name.

In this section, the Tetragrammaton is linked with *Elōhīm* in the compound expression Yhwh *Elōhīm*. This fact is easily explicable on the basis that Scripture wishes to teach us that Yhwh, who is mentioned here for the first time, is to be completely identified with *Elōhīm*, mentioned in the preceding section; in other words, that the God of the ethical world is none other than the God of the physical world, that the God of Israel is the God of the entire universe, that the names Yhwh and *Elōhīm* point only to two different aspects of His activity, or to two different ways in which He reveals Himself to the children of men. Having imparted this teaching here, there is no need to reiterate it later; hence, in the subsequent chapters, the Bible uses either the Tetragrammaton or *Elōhīm* alone, according to the context.

Now the connection between the section of the Creation and that of the Garden of Eden resembles, to a certain extent, the relationship between the two parts of Psalm xix (*The heavens are telling the glory of God*), which are not separate psalms, as most modern commentators imagine, but parallel passages linked together by a thought similar to that which unites the two benedictions preceding the reading of the morning Shema, a concept that apparently was traditional among Jews. In the first part, the poet declares God's praise as the Creator of the *physical light* and uses the name *El*; in the second, he lauds Him as the Source of the *moral light* of the Torah, and there he employs the Tetragrammaton.

When the first woman voices, on giving birth to her firstborn, her heart's joy at having become a partner of the Almighty in the work of creation, and feels, as a result of this partnership, God's personal nearness to herself, she uses, in accordance with our rules, the name Yhwh, and cries exultingly: *I have created a man equally with God* (Gen. iv 1). On the other hand, at the birth of her third son, when she is in mourning for the calamity that bereaved her of her first two sons in one day, she is indeed conscious of the power of the Creator, who fructifies and multiplies His creatures, but in the despair of her soul, which still grieves for the first two children, and with their memory revivified just at this hour, she is unable to rise to a sense of God's nearness and of sharing in His creativity. This time she does not describe the birth of her son as a new act of creation that she herself had achieved jointly with Yhwh, but as a passive acceptance on her part of what the God of life had given her: *For ʾElōhīm has appointed for me another child instead of Abel, for Cain slew him* (iv 25). The position is not unlike that depicted in Amos (vi 10) with reference to those who converse in the house of the departed: *Hush! We must not mention the name of* Yhwh. Only when the first human pair were granted to see grandchildren—a new assurance of continued life for generations—only then did they find solace and feel again the proximity of Yhwh: *Then men began once more to call upon the name of* Yhwh (Gen. iv 26).

In connection with the sacrifices of Cain and Abel (iv 3, 4) the Tetragrammaton is used because oblations can be offered up only to a personal God. The Talmudic sages already rightly noted in this regard that "in connection with none of the sacrifices mentioned in the Torah is *ʾElōhīm* or *ʾElōhekhā* ["your God"] or *Šadday* ["Almighty"] or *Ṣebbāʾōth* ["Hosts"] found, only the specific name ה״י Yhwh is used" (Sifre Num. § 143, and parallel passages). The exception to this usage in Exodus xviii 12 is intended to stress the fact that it was a stranger who brought the offering, and that, notwithstanding what is stated in the previous verse, he had not yet attained complete knowledge of the Lord, Yhwh.

In the continuation of the story of Cain and Abel (Gen. iv 6-16), God appears in an ethical role and consequently it is necessary that the Tetragrammaton should be used, and in fact it is.

The expressions *in the likeness of ʾElōhīm* and *walked with ʾElōhīm* (v 1, 22, 24) become clear to us once we realize that it would have been irreverent to write *in the likeness of* Yhwh or *walked with* Yнwн (in connection with the Tetragrammaton, Scripture prefers the phrase *walk before*, for instance, xxiv 40: Yнwн, BEFORE *whom I walk*; it would obviously have been improper to say: Yнwн, *with* whom I walk). Then, since verse 24 began with *Elōhīm*, it also concluded with that Name.

The Tetragrammaton occurs in the utterance of Noah's father, Lamech (*which* Yнwн *has cursed*), because it contains an allusion to the curse on the ground that was pronounced by Yнwн, as is stated earlier (iii 17; the subject of *said* is Yнwн *Elōhīm*, mentioned in verse 14).

As regards the phrase *the sons of Elōhīm* (vi 2, 4), it is superfluous to state that it is quite unthinkable, whatever be the meaning of this expression, for the Tetragrammaton to be used in conjunction with *sons*. It is only in antithesis to *the sons of Elōhīm* that the personal name of the One God appropriately appears in verse 3.

All those factors that we enumerated in connection with the account of Creation likewise postulated the use of *Elōhīm* in the story of the Flood; and this is the Name that the Torah actually employs throughout almost the entire narrative. When the Tetragrammaton does appear occasionally, there is a special reason for this, as I shall explain presently. But possibly we have to add here to the aforementioned factors also the intention to underline the parallel between the covenant made with Adam, the original progenitor of mankind, and the covenant entered into with Noah, the father of renascent humanity after the Deluge. The divine name mentioned in the story of the first man was the one required in the account of Noah, too, in order to tell us that this second covenant was only the continuation and renewal of the earlier one, and that the blessing given to Noah and his sons in the name of *Elōhīm* was but the fulfillment of the benison bestowed in that Name on Adam and his sons.

Also the verses in the narrative of the Flood in which the Tetragrammaton occurs conform exactly, as I have already indicated, to our rules. The name YHWH appears when the moral motive, which extends indeed through the whole story, is accorded special prominence and emphasis, as in the punishment of the wicked on account of their wickedness and in the prosperity of Noah because of his righteousness (vi 5-8; vii 1); so, too, when reference is made to the sacrifices, or to the clean animals that Noah was commanded to take with him into the Ark for the purpose of bringing oblations from them after the Flood (vii 5; viii 20-21); likewise when it is intended to express a direct—as it were, palpable—relationship between God and Noah, the relationship of a father full of compassion towards his son, who is dear to his heart (vii 16: *and* YHWH *shut him in*); similarly when Scripture reverts to the curse upon the ground (viii 21), which is mentioned in the section that uses the Tetragrammaton. In these verses we find the name YHWH; in the rest of the account of the Deluge, *'Elōhīm* occurs for the reasons given.

When Noah blesses Shem and Japhet, he mentions the Tetragrammaton in connection with the former (ix 26) and *'Elōhīm* with reference to the latter (ix 27). This points to the knowledge of YHWH, which was destined to be preserved among the descendants of Shem—it may be that even in ancient times legends were current concerning the righteousness of Shem the son of Noah and his erudition in the Torah of YHWH, similar to the later stories recorded in rabbinic literature—whereas among the sons of Japhet, even those who would succeed in rising above the conventional pagan cults would only be able to attain a general conception of God.

Of Nimrod it is written (x 9): *He was a mighty hunter before* YHWH; *therefore it is said, 'Like Nimrod a mighty hunter before* YHWH.' The words *therefore it is said* indicate that a popular proverb is quoted here: when the children of Israel wished to say that a certain person was a mighty hunter, they would compare him to *Nimrod a mighty hunter before* Yhwh. Although the content of the traditions concerning Nimrod is non-national, yet the aphorism itself is an Israelite folk saying, and we have already seen that the ordinary people, in contradistinction to the scribes, were accustomed to use the Tetragrammaton constantly in their daily speech; the Torah cites the proverb in its exact form. As for the first half of the verse, which is connected with this dictum, it was appropriate that its characteristic wording should be echoed, including the Tetragrammaton.

In the story of the Generation of Division (xi 1-9) Yhwh appears. The reason is clear: in this narrative only the place of the occurrence is outside the Land of Israel; the story itself is wholly Israelite in character, and it contains not an iota of foreign material. Unlike the accounts of the Creation and the Flood, it has no cosmopolitan tradition as its background to serve as the basis of the Torah's portrayal; on the contrary, here we find the Israelite spirit in complete opposition to the attitude and aspirations of the proud heathen peoples, who dominate the world. Thus the Israelite conception of the relationship between man and God is conveyed by the Israelite name of the Deity.

In chapter xii f., the Bible begins to relate the history of the patriarch Abraham, the founder of the people of Israel; it is fitting, therefore, that the Israelite name for the Godhead should be used here regularly. In God's revelations to Abraham, which constitute the first stage of the selection of Israel as the treasured people, in the trials to which Abraham was subjected, and in the paternal providence that grants him Heaven's protection in reward for his devotion to this God, the Deity appears in the character peculiar to the *God of Israel*, which finds expression, as we have seen, in the Tetragrammaton. Now in agreement with this, we find in a whole series of narratives about Abraham and his family, extending from the beginning of chapter xii to the end of chapter xvi, only the name YHWH.

Although the section of the Circumcision (ch. xvii) also opens with the Tetragrammaton, the name *'Elōhīm* occurs subsequently. The reason for this will become apparent as soon as we consider the content of God's words in this passage. In the first utterance, cited in the name of *'Elōhīm* (*vv*. 4-8), Abram-Abraham is promised that he will become *the father of a multitude of nations*; and Scripture proceeds to emphasize this divine promise by reverting to it in each of the first three verses of the communication (*v*. 4: *and you shall be the father of a multitude of nations*; *v*. 5: *for I have made you the father of a multitude of nations*; *v*. 6: *and I will make nations of you*). Manifestly, in connection with this assurance the appropriate divine name was not the one specific to Israel alone, but that which was also common to the other nations. The second utterance (*vv*. 9-14) concerns particularly the precept of circumcision; here, too, the name *'Elōhīm* was required, since this commandment is incumbent not only on Israel but on all the sons of Abraham, including Ishmael, the sons of Keturah and the sons of Edom. In the third address (*vv*. 15-16), the use of the name *'Elōhīm* is likewise justified since we are told with regard to Sarai-Sarah: *and she shall be a mother of nations, kings of peoples shall come from her*. For the same reason, this name is correct in the duologue that follows (*vv*. 18-21) on the subject of Ishmael and the nation that will issue from him. The same applies to the closing verses (22-23), which are connected with the preceding passage and relate how Abraham circumcised Ishmael and the slaves born in his house. The fact that also in the verses that promise Abraham the possession of the Land, and which accordingly appertain to Israel alone, there is found the name *'Elōhīm*—*v*. 7: *to be God* [*'Elōhīm*] *to you*; *v.* 8: *and I shall be their God* [*ʾElōhīm*]—constitutes no difficulty. There is no contradiction here, for it is clear that in these expressions the name *ʾElōhīm* is purely a common noun, and the thought is that Yhwh, who had appeared to Abraham, as is stated in *v.* 1, and who is designated *ʾElōhīm* in relation to the other nations, will become *Israel's God*, the *specific God* of Israel. In such phrases even the prophets employ the name *ʾElōhīm*; for example, Ezekiel xxxvii 27: *and I will be their God* [*ʾElōhīm*], *and they shall be My people*. It is perfectly clear that the name *ʾElōhīm*, which forms a parallel here to *people*, is, like the latter, a general substantive.

In the section of the Circumcision, the name *ʾElōhīm* serves also to emphasize the parallelism between Abraham and Noah and Adam. Ten generations after the original progenitor of humanity, Noah arose—a wholly righteous man, who walked with God in the midst of a generation that was altogether wicked, and, on account of his righteousness, was saved from the universal retribution and became the father of all mankind after the Flood. Ten generations after Noah came Abraham, who also was alone in recognizing his Creator in a generation that was estranged from Him, and because of his righteousness was chosen to be the physical ancestor of the treasured people and the spiritual father of all mankind; and he was enjoined, in words similar to those used of Noah: *Walk before Me and be wholehearted*. The covenant made with him and the blessing bestowed upon him by God are depicted here as the completion and the crown of the covenant and benison that were given to the first man. Even the phrases are similar, and the correspondence of phraseology is indicative of the parallelism of content. To Adam God said: *Be fruitful and multiply, and fill the earth* (Gen. i 28), and to Noah He likewise said: *Be fruitful and multiply, and fill the earth* (ix 1), and thereafter: *be fruitful and multiply, bring forth abundantly on the earth and multiply in it* (ix 7); and to Abraham He said, adding the repeated adverb בִּמְאֹד מְאֹד *bimeʾōdh meʾōdh* ["exceedingly"]: *and I will multiply you exceedingly... and I will make you exceedingly fruitful* (xvii 2, 6). Of his sons it is subsequently said: *and were fruitful and multiplied exceedingly* (xlvii 27); and again: *But the descendants of Israel were fruitful and increased greatly; they multiplied and grew exceedingly strong; so the land was filled with them* (Exod. i 7). Not only were they *fruitful* but they also *increased greatly*; not only did they multiply but, moreover, they grew strong; exceedingly—as it was said to Abraham; so the land was filled with them—as it was promised to Adam and Noah. A "sign of a covenant" was given to Noah (Gen. ix 12, 13, 17) and the "sign of a covenant" is required of Abraham (xvii 11: *and it shall be a sign of a covenant between Me and you*—the very words of ix 13: *and it shall be a sign of the covenant between Me and the earth*). In the earlier passage it is written: *Behold, I establish My covenant with you and your descendants after you* (ix 9), and here it is stated: *And I will establish My covenant between Me and you and your descendants after you* (xvii 7); both there (ix 16) and here (xvii 7, 13, 19) reference is made to *an everlasting covenant*; there we read: *On the very same day* (vii 13), and likewise here (xvii 23, 26); there we are told: *that never again shall all flesh* BE CUT OFF *by the waters of the flood* (ix 11)—an assurance that the covenant would be fulfilled on God's part, and here: *that soul shall* BE CUT OFF *from his people* (xvii 14)—the punishment that would befall any descendant of Abraham who would fail to fulfil the covenant. If we wish to gain a thorough understanding of the passages, we must take note of recapitulations and allusions of this kind, because they were certainly not unpremeditated. These parallels do not resemble in the least the stylistic and linguistic parallels on which the protagonists of the documentary hypothesis rely, as I shall explain in my next lecture. They are rather like those on which the rabbinic sages used to comment, mostly for homiletical purposes, but sometimes with profound insight into the real meaning of the text.

I believe that there is no need for me to continue this analysis further. One could easily proceed to review the remaining sections and show how the name *Elōhīm* is used, for instance, when the reference is to an alien people (xix 29: the beginning of the story of the origin of the children of Moab and Ammon; xxi 8-21: Ishmael's departure from his father's house and the founding of his own family); or when God reveals Himself to a member of the gentile nations (xx 3, 6: God manifests Himself to Abimelech; xxxi 24: He manifests Himself to Laban) or in conversations with gentiles (xx 11, 13; xxi 22, 23, and so on and so forth); or when there is any other reason from among those that we have enumerated; and, on the other hand, that the Tetragrammaton occurs when required by the aforementioned rules (needless to say, even non-Israelites use the name YHWH when they have in mind the specific God worshipped by the patriarchs, for example, xxvi 28, 29; xxx 27). It would be easy to prolong the list of citations, but just because it is easy it is also superfluous.[1] If you examine the remaining sections, you will be convinced that the variations in the use of the names YHWH and *Elōhīm* can always be explained without difficulty on the basis of the rules that we have set forth.

There is no reason, therefore, to feel surprise that the use of these names varies in the Torah. On the contrary, we should be surprised if they were not changed about. The position is of necessity what it is. It is not a case of disparity between different documents, or of mechanical amalgamation of separate texts; every Hebrew author was compelled to write thus and to use the two Names in this manner, because their primary signification, the general literary tradition of the ancient East, and the rules governing the use of the divine names throughout the entire range of Hebrew literature, demanded this.

From this it follows that the first of the five pillars on which the proud structure of the documentary hypothesis rests—its central pillar—cannot withstand a thoroughgoing examination of its material and stability. When the hand of investigation touches it, it crumbles and turns to dust.

Now we must test the remaining pillars; and to their examination I wish to dedicate the coming lectures.

LANGUAGE AND STYLE

TODAY WE SHALL TURN our attention to the second pillar, to the variations in language and style, that is, to the divergences between one section and another in respect of vocabulary, grammatical forms and diction in general.[1] We shall endeavor to clarify the nature of this pillar and to probe its value.

As I explained in the opening lecture of this course, the first attempt, made by Witter, to conjecture the principal documents that served as the basis of the Pentateuch did not achieve great publicity, and it was soon forgotten; whereas Astruc, who lived approximately forty years after Witter and expressed views similar to his, was regarded as a path-finder and came to be called "the father of the documentary hypothesis." Astruc's success was particularly due to the fact that the German savant Eichhorn agreed with his theories and developed them in accordance with sound scientific methods, studying them more deeply and perfecting them with the help of the professional erudition at the command of a scholar of his caliber.

Eichhorn was not content to determine which paragraphs were to be attributed in his opinion to each of the principal documents;

he also endeavored to ascertain, in exact detail, the specific characteristics of the documents, particularly from the linguistic aspect.
Eichhorn held that each document had its own linguistic character, which found expression in special features of the lexicographi-
cal material, in the grammatical construction and in its stylistic
peculiarities. After him, too, scholars devoted much attention to
the subject and continued to investigate it in all its details with
exceeding acumen, deducing thereby endless critical rules. Long
and comprehensive lists of words and grammatical forms peculiar to each of the main sources were drawn up. Although latterly work in this field no longer occupies scholars to the same
extent as before, yet this must not be interpreted as indicating a
desire on the part of exegetes to refrain from a type of research
that has lost its value in view of new trends; but on the contrary,
it implies a kind of assent, at all events in general principle, to
what previous investigators had already achieved, as though all the
work that could be done in this direction had already been successfully accomplished, and there was nothing left for us to do
today but to accept the results of these labors—or at least those
conclusions that seemed most assured—as a firm and enduring
basis of scholarship.

In truth anyone with intelligence will observe that differences
of the kinds mentioned actually do exist between given sections,
and these give rise to questions calling for an answer. We find in
one passage, for instance, *so-and-so* הוֹלִיד *hōlīdh* [*Hiph'īl*; "begot"]
so-and-so, and in another, *so-and-so* יָלַד *yāladh* [*Qal*; "begot"] *so-
and-so*. Why this divergency? The answer given by the proponents
of the documentary hypothesis is as follows: If we find in some
places *hōlīdh* and in others *yāladh*, this indicates that we have
before us fragments taken from various documents, which differ
in the use of this verb; one source employs it in the *Hiph'īl* and
the other in the *Qal*, even in *Hiph'īl* senses. This conclusion,
they add, helps us again in two other directions: (a) it provides

us with evidence of the correctness of our hypothesis concerning the existence of various sources; (b) it opens the way for us to determine the provenance of those passages that would otherwise have remained in doubt: if we are able, for example, to decide that the source using *yāladh* in the *Qal* is J, and that employing *hōlīdh* in the *Hiph'īl* is P, it follows from this that every text in which the *Qal* is found in the meaning of the *Hiph'īl* emanates from source J, and every passage in which the *Hiph'īl* occurs is derived from source P.

Generally speaking this appears to be an acceptable argument. In regard to the first point, that it furnishes proof of the existence of various documents, there can be no doubt that as a rule the same author does not change his linguistic usages from chapter to chapter in the course of his book. As for the second point, that the source of a given passage can be identified on the basis of its linguistic features, this, too, is correct: use of the same phraseology can be an indication of the same source of origin. The objection raised by several scholars that in using this argument we are constantly reasoning in a circle, founding our conclusions on the very thing we set out to prove, is not justified, or at least is not always justified.

All this is true in general principle. But when we consider the matter more closely, we see that in reality it is not quite so simple as it appears on the surface. With regard to point one, it is essential, if we wish to avoid hasty and erroneous deductions, that we should first prove that the differences cited actually constitute a linguistic change, that is, to revert to the previous example, we must establish that the *Hiph'īl* "*hōlīdh*" and the *Qal* "*yāladh*" belong to two distinct linguistic schools, and that it is impossible for them to be used together. Concerning the second argument, it is not only necessary that we should furnish the proof we mentioned in regard to the first point, but we must also eschew three things: (a) we must not rely upon the differences in language in order to determine the origin of the sections, which we shall subsequently use to decide the linguistic characteristics of the sources, for in that case we shall indeed fall into the snare of reasoning in a circle; (b) nor emend the texts in order to make them conform to our theory; (c) nor consider words and forms mechanically, as though they were divorced from their context and the latter could have no bearing on their use. As we shall soon see, the exponents of the documentary hypothesis were not always careful to avoid all these pitfalls.

But it is not my intention to dwell any longer on questions of general principle. The best way to elucidate the subject is to study the passages in detail without any bias whatsoever, and to determine the exact value of the relevant words and forms. This is the task to which I dedicated the second part of *La Questione*, mentioned earlier, and I intend to recapitulate this work with you today.

It is obvious that we shall not be able to traverse all the ground that I covered at length in that volume. There will not be sufficient time for this, nor is it necessary for the purpose of these lectures. I shall be content to put before you, with extreme brevity, a few examples that will clearly demonstrate my method and the general conclusions to which it leads; whoever wishes to study the subject further and more deeply can consult my book directly. I shall choose the illustrative passages from among those that are considered even today among the clearest and strongest proofs of the documentary hypothesis.

First of all let us consider the peculiarity to which I have already referred today, to wit, the divergent use of *yāladh* in the *Qal* and of *hōlīdh* in the *Hiph'īl*. The rule formulated by the adherents of the documentary hypothesis is, as I have stated, that the verb *yāladh* in the *Qal*, which is normally used *in relation to the mother* (so-and-so *gave birth* to so-and-so), does not occur with reference to the father, that is, in the sense of *hōlīdh* ["begot"], except in source J alone; whereas document P uses only *hōlīdh* in this sense. It is stated in the genealogy of Cain (Gen. iv 18): *And unto Enoch was born Irad; and Irad begot [yāladh] Mehujael, and Mehijael begot [yāladh] Methushael, and Methushael begot [yāladh] Lamech.* In the pedigree of Nahor (xxii 23) we find: *and Bethuel begot [yāladh] Rebekah.* Both these passages are ascribed to J; so, too, are the verses in the genealogy of the seventy nations (ch. x) that contain the verb *yāladh* in the *Qal.* On the other hand, in the list of the ten generations from Adam to Noah (ch. v), and in that of the ten generations from Noah to Abraham (xi 10-26), both of which are attributed to P, the *Hiph'īl* is always used, for example: *And the days of Adam after* HE BEGOT [*hōlīdhō*] *Seth were eight hundred years*; AND HE BEGOT [*wayyōledh*] *sons and daughters* (v 4), and so on. Here then is the distinction between the two documents, J on the one hand and P on the other.

But the whole argument is open to a number of objections. The Tetragrammaton, the unmistakable sign of source J, does not occur at all in the genealogy of Cain, only in the preceding story of Cain and Abel, and the exponents of the documentary theory could easily, in accordance with their method of reasoning, have separated the passages and asserted, had they any cause to do so, that Cain's pedigree did not belong to the same source as the previous narrative. But, on the contrary, they connect the genealogy with the narrative and attribute them to J for reasons of their own, including the fact that they use *yāladh*. This is also one of the factors that prompt them to ascribe Nahor's family tree to J. In the case of the aforementioned verses in the genealogy of the seventy nations, this is actually the decisive reason. We thus have here a clear and typical instance of reasoning in a circle: first these passages are attributed to J because they contain *yāladh*; thereafter the deduction is made that *yāladh* is an expression peculiar to J.

Furthermore, the verb *yāladh* in the *Qal* occurs a number of times in the Bible in the signification of *hōlīdh*, even in poetry (for example: *You were unmindful of the Rock that* BEGOT YOU [*yelādhᵉkhā*], Deut. xxxii 18); and even outside the Pentateuch, for instance, Hos. v 7: *They have dealt faithlessly with the Lord; for they have begotten* [*yālādhū*] *alien children*; so, too, Psalms (ii 7), Proverbs (xvii 21; xxiii 22, 24), and Job (xxxviii 29). There can be no doubt, therefore, that the usage is not restricted to any particular linguistic section.

The *Hiph'īl* "*hōlīdh*," even more so, cannot be regarded as characteristic of any special linguistic group; it is the normal expression for "begetting" in the Bible and throughout the entire range of Hebrew usage, as all Hebrew-speaking persons are well aware. It will thus be seen that the documentary theory does not solve the problem of the difference between the sections that use *yāladh* and those that employ *hōlīdh*. Is it possible to find another solution that is acceptable? Indeed it is possible.

It will suffice to note the fact that the verb *yāladh* occurs in the signification of *hōlīdh* only in the *past tense* [perfect] and the *present* [participle]. We say, "so-and-so *yāladh* [mas. sing. perfect] so-and-so," and we say *yōlēdh* [participle mas. sing.; "is begetting"]; but we do not say in the *future tense* [imperfect] "so-and-so *yēlēdh* [to signify: "he will beget"] (or *wayyēledh* [imperfect with *wāw* conversive, to connote: "and he begot"]) so-and-so." In the imperfect, the *Qal* is employed only with reference to the mother, for example, "so-and-so *tēlēdh* ["will give birth to"] (or *wattēledh* ["and gave birth to"]) so-and-so." In connection with the father one can only say, *yōlīdh* [*Hiph'īl* imperfect; "he will beget"] or *wayyōledh* [*Hiph'īl* imperfect with *wāw* conversive; "and he begot"] (although we find in Prov. xxvii 1: *what a day may bring forth* ["*yēledh*"; *Qal* imperfect] the verb is used there not in the connotation of "begetting" but actually in the sense of "giving birth"). Similarly, we do not say, using the infinitive, *'aḥărē lidhtō* [to signify: "after his begetting"] but only *'aḥărē lidhtāh* ["after her giving birth"]; with regard to the father we can only say, *'aḥărē hōlīdhō* ["after his begetting"]. This is clear to anyone who is sensitive to the Hebrew idiom. In the genealogies from Adam to Noah and from Noah to Abraham, it would have been impossible to write anything else but *wayyōledh* and *ʾaḥărē hōlīdhō*; every Hebrew author would have had no option but to write thus and not otherwise. It is not a question of sources but of the general usages of the Hebrew tongue.

As for the past tense, in which it is permissible to use both *yāladh* and *hōlīdh*, all depends on the sequence of the verses. When a passage commences with *wayyiwwāledh* ["and he was born"] in the *Niphʿal*, which has more affinity with the *Qal*, or when it has the *Qal* at the beginning with reference to the mother, for example, *yāledhā* ["she gave birth"], then the text is inclined to continue in the *Qal*, employing *yāladh* also for the masculine. But when the text opens with the verb in the *Hiphʿīl*, for instance, *wayyōledh*, or with the substantive *tōledhōth*, which is related to the *Hiphʿīl*, it continues in the *Hiphʿīl* even in the past tense, using *hōlīdh*. (I do not wish to bore you by quoting all the verses relevant to the subject; you can examine them by yourselves.) Thus the whole position becomes clear. We are dealing not with linguistic idiosyncrasies peculiar to various sources, but with general rules of the language, which apply equally to all writers and all books.

A second example. The concept of *making a covenant* between God and man is expressed, according to the documentary hypothesis, in source P by the idiom הֵקִים בְּרִית *hēqīm berīth* ["He established a covenant"] (sometimes by נָתַן בְּרִית *nāthan berīth* ["He gave a covenant"]), and in other sources by the usual phrase כָּרַת בְּרִית *kārath berīth* [literally, "He cut a covenant"]. This thesis is accepted as an unquestionable fact, and all who are engaged in biblical research reiterate it, one after the other, without ever thinking of testing it and seeing whether or not it corresponds to the actual textual position. Yet this test is by no means superfluous. If we examine the passages carefully, we shall see that the

idioms *hēqīm bᵉrīth* and *kārath bᵉrīth* are not identical in meaning. "To cut a covenant" signifies to give a certain assurance; "to
establish a covenant" connotes the actual fulfillment of an assurance that had been given at the time of the making of the covenant. They thus refer to two different matters, and are not different expressions for the same idea. For example: in the section
of the Circumcision (Gen. xvii), after the declaration, *As for Me,
behold My covenant is with you* (*v.* 4), it is further stated, AND I
WILL ESTABLISH [*wahăqīmōthī*] *My covenant between Me and you,
and your descendants after you throughout their generations* (*v.* 7).
Wahăqīmōthī is past tense [perfect] with *wāw* conversive, signifying the future. Seeing, however, that the covenant exists already
in the present (*v.* 4), is it necessary to make another covenant in
the future? Obviously, the meaning here is: I shall actually fulfill
My covenant, in you and your descendants after you throughout
the generations. The subsequent statement in the same section
is even clearer. Abraham hears with misgiving the promise that
a son will be born to him from Sarah; he fears for Ishmael, his
first son born of Hagar, and he says: *Oh that Ishmael might live
in Thy sight* (*v.* 18). God answers him: *No, but Sarah your wife
shall bear you a son, and you shall call his name Isaac.* I WILL ES-
TABLISH [*wahăqīmōthī*] *My covenant with him* (*v.* 19), the meaning being: in him shall be *fulfilled* the promise that I have given
you; *As for Ishmael, I have heard you, behold I will bless him... and
I will make him a great nation. But My covenant* I WILL ESTAB-
LISH [*ʾāqīm*] *with Isaac* (*vv.* 20-21), that is, although My blessing
will also be bestowed on Ishmael, yet My covenant, My promise
for the generations to come, I shall *fulfill in Isaac.* This is also
clear from the other passages, which I do not, however, intend
to cite seriatim. In this case, too, then, we are dealing not with
fragments of various sources that use different expressions for one
idea, but with two separate, unrelated conceptions, each of which
finds expression through its proper idiom. When we wish to say

that a promise was given, we use the expression *kārath berīth*, and when we wish to state that the assurance was fulfilled, we use the term *hēqīm berīth*.

Example three. The exponents of the documentary hypothesis think that source E uses the phrase "to bring up from Egypt," whereas source J employs the expression "to bring forth from Egypt." Let us also examine this divergency. These two idioms are indeed of kindred meaning, but they are not completely identical. When I say: The Lord *brought up* the children of Israel from Egypt, that is, that He *brought them up* from the valley of the Nile to the mountains of Israel, I have in mind the entry into the Land, the final *goal* that the children of Israel reached. On the other hand, when I say that the Lord *brought forth* the Israelites from Egypt, I convey only the idea of *going forth* from the house of bondage, of passing beyond the borders of Egypt, of being liberated from the servitude, without any reference to the ultimate destination. Whether the first or second expression is used depends on the requirements of the theme. When Jacob is about to leave the land of Canaan and go down to Egypt, and he is anxious about the future possession of the Land, since he is leaving it together with his family, the word of God comes to comfort and assure him: *I will also* SURELY BRING YOU UP *again* (Gen. xlvi 4); that is, I shall bring you *hither* again, to this land: it is an answer to his fears concerning the possession of the Land.

The same applies to Joseph's words to his brethren: *and He will bring you up out of this land to the land which He swore to Abraham, to Isaac and to Jacob* (1 24). Here the entry into the country is specifically mentioned, and this is the very point that Joseph has in mind. Continuing, he says: *and you shall bring* [E.V. "carry"] *up my bones from here*. What is of importance to Joseph is not merely that they should *take* his bones *out* of Egyptian territory, but that they should *bring* them *up* to the land of Canaan.

Conversely, in the Covenant of the Pieces it is written: *and also that nation, whom they shall serve, will I judge, and afterward they shall go forth with great possessions* (xv 14). Here the point is simply the antithesis between the bondage (*whom they shall serve*) and the liberation: although they will enslave your children, yet afterwards the latter shall *go forth* and cease to be under their oppressors' yoke. The entry into the Land is mentioned later: *and they* SHALL COME BACK *in the fourth generation*, etc. (*v.* 16). If we refrain from dealing with the verses mechanically, and endeavor to penetrate their inner meaning, the underlying principle becomes clear to us, so clear that it seems to me superfluous to quote any further passages.

A further example: the difference between the personal pronouns אֲנִי *ănī* and אָנֹכִי *ānōkhī* ["I"]. The two sources, J and E, according to the protagonists of the documentary hypothesis, prefer *ānōkhī*, whereas P, on the other hand, uses only *ănī*. In P *ănī* is found approximately one hundred and thirty times, whilst *ānōkhī* occurs only once, in the verse, I [*ānōkhī*] *am a stranger and a sojourner among you* (xxiii 4). However, all such numbers, as well as all the statistical tables that have been drawn up to show the difference between the sources, fail to prove the case. In these tables the pronouns are cited as though they were completely divorced from their context, no attention being paid to the various syntactic forms and the particular idioms in which they are found. For instance, the expression *ănī* YHWH ["I am the Lord"] occurs innumerable times, but since this is a stereotyped phrase that never varies in form, all these examples are equal to little more than one case. Furthermore, in view of the fact that the word *ānōkhī* is composed of three syllables and *ănī* of only one (in pausal form אָנִי *ănī*, which has two syllables), they differ in their effect on the rhythm of the sentence, and it is possibly this distinction that is responsible for the choice of the first or second

word according to circumstances. It is worthwhile examining the
biblical text in order to see if this conjecture is justified or not.
I have already investigated for this purpose all the verses in the
Book of Genesis that contain one of the two pronouns, and I am
convinced that this is actually the case. Following are the results
of my study in detail:

(a) If the pronoun is the subject of a verbal clause, that is,
of a clause containing a verb in the past [perfect] or in the future [imperfect], irrespective of whether the pronoun precedes the
verb or vice versa, *ānōkhī* is used, for example: I [*ānōkhī*] *gave
my maid to your embrace* (xvi 5); *and even I* [*ānōkhī*] *may have
children* [literally, "may be built up"] *through her* (xxx 3). This is
the invariable rule, except in one instance (xiv 23: I [*ănī*] *have
made Abram rich*), where the sentence is unusual in its word-
rhythm, having a *Metheg* in the first syllable of the verb [*heˁĕšartī*,
"I made rich"].

(b) When the pronoun is part of a compound subject (others
and *I*), and follows the verb, it is always *ănī*, for instance: *hăbhōˀ
nābhōˀ *ănī* weˁimmekhā weˀaḥekhā* ["Shall I and your mother and
your brothers indeed come"] (xxxvii 10).

(c) When the pronoun is *nominativus pendens* at the beginning of the sentence, and the subject of the sentence appertains
to the speaker, *ănī* is invariably employed, for example: AS FOR
ME [*ănī*], *behold My covenant is with you* (xvii 4); but if someone
else is the subject, the pronoun is *ānōkhī*: AS FOR ME [*ānōkhī*],
the Lord has led me in the way (xxiv 27).

(d) If the pronoun is not the subject, but comes to emphasize
the pronominal suffix of the preceding verb, it is invariably *ănī*:
Bless ME [*ănī*] *also* (xxvii 34, 38).

(e) In noun clauses, that is, in those that have no verb in the
past [perfect] or in the future [imperfect], if it is desired to emphasize the subject, the pronoun is *ānōkhī*, for example: *Fear not,*

Abram, I [*ănōkhī*] *am* [the verb is understood] *your shield* (xv 1);
but if the Bible does not wish to stress the subject, or it desires
to give greater emphasis to the object, the pronoun is *ănī*, for
example: I [*ănī*] REMEMBER *my faults today* (xli 9).

Having determined the fact that the use of the two pronouns
depends on rules that are the same for the entire book in all
its sections, be the source to which they are customarily attributed what it may, it is clear that the variations in the use of the
Names are due not to change of source, but to general linguistic
reasons only.

An interesting example is furnished by the words טֶרֶם *ṭerem*
and בְּטֶרֶם *beṭerem*. It is usually stated that source E employs the
expression *beṭerem*, and that J prefers *ṭerem*, without *bēth*; consequently all verses in which *beṭerem* occurs are to be ascribed to E,
and all those in which *ṭerem* appears, to J. But this is a mistaken
view. These are not two expressions of identical signification, which
can be interchanged at will. *Beṭerem* means one thing, and *ṭerem*
another. *Ṭerem* is an adverb and connotes *not yet*, for example: *Do
you* NOT YET [*ṭerem*] *understand that Egypt is ruined?* (Exod. x 7);
whereas *beṭerem* is a conjunction, signifying *before*, for instance:
that I may bless you BEFORE [*beṭerem*] *I die* (Gen. xxvii 4). It is
obvious that, since the connotation of the two words is different, each one is used in accordance with the meaning required.
Thus there is no question here of different sources but of a rule
equally applicable to every Hebrew writer and to every Hebrew
book. It would have been quite impossible for anyone to write:
"*habheṭerem tēdha* [to signify: 'Do you not yet understand'] that
Egypt is ruined?"; nor could one say: "that I may bless you *ṭerem*
ămūth [to connote: 'before I die']."

Permit me to cite a final illustration: the variations in the order of the numerals. In biblical Hebrew, as we know, it is possible to arrange the compound numerals in two different ways:

sometimes the units precede the tens, and the tens the hundreds, and the hundreds the thousands; on the other hand, at times the thousands come before the hundreds, and the hundreds before the tens, and the tens before the units. For instance, we find *a hundred and twenty* in descending order, and also *twenty and a hundred* in ascending order; *forty and five* occurs, and also *five and forty*. The prevailing view in this regard is that the difference between the descending and ascending orders is due to a difference of sources: it is held that documents J, E and D almost always employed the descending order, whilst P preferred as a rule the ascending order. And it is indeed a fact that in the section attributed to P, the rising order is found as a rule, and in the other sections nearly always the descending order occurs. At first sight, this appears a surprising peculiarity; but only at first sight. When we examine the passages carefully, we see that the position is totally different from what is generally believed. Upon investigating all the compound numbers in the Bible, I discovered that the ascending and descending orders are used according to definite rules that hold good for all the books.

This is the principal rule: when the Bible gives us technical or statistical data and the like, it frequently prefers the ascending order, since the tendency to exactness in these instances causes the smaller numbers to be given precedence and prominence. On the other hand, when a solitary number occurs in a narrative passage or in a poem or in a speech and so forth, the numbers are invariably arranged, save in a few cases where special circumstances operate, according to the more natural and spontaneous order, to wit, the descending order. This is a fundamental rule governing the use of the numerals in Hebrew. We read, for example, in the story of the sons of God and the daughters of men: *but his days shall be* A HUNDRED AND TWENTY *years* (Gen. vi 3); so, too, in Moses' address to the children of Israel before his death: *I am*

A HUNDRED AND TWENTY *years old this day* (Deut. xxxi 2); and similarly it is related subsequently: *and Moses was* A HUNDRED AND TWENTY *years old when he died* (xxxiv 7); it is further recorded in the Book of Kings: *Hiram had sent to the king* ONE HUNDRED AND TWENTY *talents of gold* (i Kings ix 14). But in the list of statistical data concerning the offerings of the princes, it is stated: *All the gold of the dishes being* TWENTY AND A HUNDRED *shekels* (Num. vii 86); and likewise of each of the princes it is said: *his offering was one silver plate whose weight was* THIRTY AND A HUNDRED *shekels* (vii 13f.). So, too, to quote a last example, in the statistical information concerning Solomon's chief officers: *These were the chief officers who were over Solomon's work* FIFTY AND FIVE HUNDRED, *who had charge of the people*, etc. (i Kings ix 23). Needless to say, beside this main rule there are other secondary rules—corollaries, as it were, of the primary principle—which serve to explain the special cases that I have mentioned; but it is not my intention to enter at this stage into details that will doubtless not interest you unduly. Whoever wishes to study them will find them in *La Questione*, where he will see how all the instances in the Bible of a rising order are explicable according to the principles that I have adumbrated. What concerns us at the moment is the fact that, since this system obtains in all the biblical books, we are permitted to conclude that there is no basis here for the assumption of divergent sources.

You may ask: But how is it possible to explain the fact that just in the sections attributed to P the ascending order is mostly to be found? The answer is simple: to P is ascribed, on the basis of the assumed character of this source, all the chronological and genealogical tables, all the statistical records, all the technical descriptions of services, and the like; the result is that the numerical order peculiar to cases of this type appears to occur more often in P. In the few narrative passages attributed to P, as in all other narratives, the descending order is followed; for example: *Abraham was* NINETY AND NINE *years when he was circumcised in the flesh of his foreskin* (Gen. xvii 24).

But we have had enough examples appertaining to the vocabulary and grammatical structure of the language. There remains for us only to say a few words on the question of style. In this regard, too, I shall not enter into details, but I shall briefly indicate the broad lines of difference between P and the other documents. It is usually stated that the style of P, in contradistinction to that of the other sources, is cold, dry and jejune; it is meticulous in respect of details and shows a fondness for stereotyped phrases, which are constantly reiterated in the identical form. In truth, the existence of these characteristics in the sections referred to P is to a certain extent an indisputable fact; whereas the style of the sections ascribed to J, for instance, or for that matter also to E, is clear and vivid, colorful and full of life; it is invariably marked by a charm of its own. But let us not be deceived by appearances. Let us not forget that to P are attributed those very sections that by their nature are necessarily dull and arid. How, for example, is it possible to infuse vitality and the distinctive charm of fine writing into genealogical records like those of the "book of the history of Adam" or the list of Shem's descendants? On the other hand, the limited number of narrative sections that are customarily allotted to P show the vividness and grace of diction that characterize the narratives attributed to J and E. Conversely, in the few instances where genealogical lists are ascribed to J, we find the same frigid, insipid and schematic manner of writing peculiar to the P genealogies. In a word, change of style depends on change of subject matter, not on difference of sources.

I shall not prolong the discussion. I believe that you have been convinced by now that all the disparities of which we have spoken today do not point to the existence of specific documents like J, E or P, and that they can all be explained simply by means of firmly established rules of the language, equally valid for all Hebrew writers and all Hebrew books.

It follows, therefore, that the second pillar likewise failed to stand up to examination. From afar it appeared as though hewn out of granite; when we drew near to it and touched it with our fingers, we realized that this stone was no better than that of the first pillar, and that like the latter it disintegrated of its own accord at a finger's touch. The second pillar, too, lies in ruins.

CONTRADICTIONS AND DIVERGENCES OF VIEW

LET US NOW APPROACH the third pillar, namely, the differences in the content of the texts, in other words, the contradictions and divergences between one section and another.[1] Yesterday we dealt with the variations of form, the external disparities; today we shall devote ourselves to the inner inconsistencies.

The proponents of the dominant theory have drawn attention to many incongruities of this kind: discrepant conceptions in the sphere of religion and ethics; disparate viewpoints in regard to modes of worship or national and political problems; indications of varying customs in the life of the community, and also explicit contradictions between two conflicting passages. It is unnecessary to add that they set great store by these differences as corroborative evidence of the correctness of their theory and as additional means of determining the sources of the texts. This then is one of the important pillars on which the structure of the documentary hypothesis rests. It is for us now to probe this pillar and to test its stability.

The task is not an easy one. The materials constituting the pillar in question are so different in character, and so great in number, that we shall certainly not be able to cover them all today. I shall, therefore, content myself today, too, with citing a few examples culled from *La Questione*; anyone wishing to pursue the study of the subject will find there the complete material.

One of the more important—perhaps, *the* most important—of the categories of inner disparities between the sources, pointed out by the scholars mentioned, concerns the conception of the Deity and His relationship to mankind. It merits our attention first.

These dissimilarities, which are particularly pronounced in the Book of Genesis, may be summarized as follows:

Document J regards Yhwh as the national God of the children of Israel and, incidentally, as the God of the world. It conceives Him as the Creator of heaven and earth, Lord of all peoples, the Leader and Judge of humanity, who judges men in righteousness according to their deeds, and who watches in particular over all those who acknowledge Him and serve Him faithfully. This source does not present Yhwh to us as an abstract Being, completely removed from the material universe, but it invests Him with personality, ascribes to Him humanlike sentiments, and describes His direct relations with the children of men—especially with His faithful followers—His acceptance of their prayers, and particularly how He reveals Himself to them in forms more or less corporeal, even in bright daylight, and sometimes through His angels.

Far different is the standpoint of source E. In these sections a more exalted theological concept finds expression, and in them the distance between man and God is greater. The theophanies in E are not marked by so great a tendency towards corporeality; indeed, this source makes no mention at all, until Moses' time, of God's having revealed Himself in daylight; and even at night, according to this document, God manifests Himself to men only in visions and dreams. When people are awake, God does not reveal Himself in Person but through the medium of angels. Even these do not appear to man upon earth, but speak to him from Heaven.

As for P, the disparity between him and J is even greater. P rises to a completely transcendental concept. The creatures are separated from the Infinite God by a deep gulf that cannot be crossed by any material bridge; one can only fly over it in a spiritual leap. Corporeal allusions are found in this source only on those rare occasions when they are needed to explain divine concepts in human terms. In P God does not reveal Himself in bodily form, or in dreams and visions, or even through the medium of angels. P merely states that God spoke with a certain person; that is all. If on occasion P also adds that God manifested Himself to a human being, or that after speaking He returned to Heaven, he does not go beyond the bounds of these general expressions, nor does he venture, in any manner whatsoever, to give us a description of the theophany.

This is how the differences between the three documents J, E and P regarding the conception of the Divine Being and the way in which He reveals Himself to human beings are customarily represented. In truth, it is indisputable that disparities do in fact exist between certain sections in regard to the conception of the Deity (I shall deal later with the manner of the divine manifestations). Possibly these divergences indicate the different types of tradition that have been absorbed into the various sections; but they do not prove the existence of documents such as J, E and P, and they contain nothing that could not be found in a homogeneous book. The fact that in the sections ascribed to J, where the name YHWH occurs, God appears in a more personal aspect and is endowed with the special attributes just mentioned, whilst in the sections allotted to E and P, which employ the name *'Elōhīm*, a more abstract concept is reflected, is quite explicable on the basis of the rules governing the use of the two divine names that we have set forth in the previous lectures. The disparity between the sections attributed to E and those ascribed to P can likewise be fully explained when we bear in mind that to E are generally referred the narrative sections with their vivid colorfulness, and to P mostly the more doctrinal passages.

Should you counter: "But even so, the fact that in the various sections different concepts of God are reflected cannot but raise doubts in our minds," then permit me to illustrate my argument with a story.

Let us imagine that a certain author writes a biography of his father, who was a notable savant, an academician. We shall assume that in this book the writer gives us a multi-faceted picture of his father, describing his private life at home, his relations with his students at college, and his scientific work. We shall also suppose that the writer does not devote a special section to each of these aspects, but arranges his material in chronological order, and in consequence so blends the passages appertaining to the three themes that each part of the book contains something relating to each one of them. Let us further presume that the pupils and admirers of this scholar and his academic circle were accustomed to call him just "the professor"; they knew full well, of course, that there were many professors in the world, but to them he was "the professor"—with the definite article. Doubtless when the author proceeds to write his work, in the passages describing his father's life within the family circle, he refers to him as "Father"; he writes, for example: "Then Father said so-and-so to Mother"; or "on that day Father arrived home feeling depressed, but his children, who came running joyfully to meet him, cheered him up." On the other hand, in the sections that portray him in the circle of his students at the university, he uses the designation by which he was generally known in that circle, to wit, "the professor"; and similarly in the sections that treat his scientific labors, his researches, inventions and discoveries.

Let us now picture to ourselves that centuries or millennia later a scholar will come and seek to determine the authorship of the book. If he adopts the methods of the documentary hypothesis, this scholar will declare: Since I observe that the hero of the work is called in some places "Father" and in others "the professor," it follows that we have here fragments culled from different writers, and the dissimilarity between the narrative and scientific sections corroborates this. On this basis, I divide the text of the volume into three categories, each of which derives from a separate source: all the passages using the name "Father" emanate from one source; those in which the usual appellation is "the professor" and their content has a narrative character are taken from source two; and those that likewise designate their hero "the professor," but have a scientific content, belong to a third source. He will then add: The three authors, it is seen, depict their hero differently. According to the first writer, he was a simple man completely devoted to his wife and children, always to be found in the circle of this family and ever concerned with its welfare; according to the second author, he was completely dedicated to teaching and to training his students in scientific work, and he always appears before his students in a manner that constantly reminds them of the distance between himself and them; the third source presents him as a man who has no direct contact whatsoever with social and family life, who is always shut up in his laboratory, among his books and instruments, and has no interest apart from scientific research. Notwithstanding the entire analysis of this scholar, we know that he is mistaken, for according to our premise there was only one author, and his whole work is a homogeneous composition. Nor does the book depict three separate persons, but three different aspects of one individual, aspects that can be found together in a single personality, since they are not mutually exclusive.

The same position obtains with regard to the Torah. It comes to teach us the various facets of the Divine Person, who is at one and the same time the God of Israel and of the gentiles; the God Most High, who transcends nature and yet is near to the heart of man and cares for him as does a father for his son; who is far removed from all corporeality but nevertheless reveals Himself to His chosen ones and enables them to hear His voice. These varied aspects are not found inconsistent by the conscience of the man of faith, who is wholehearted with his God, and is convinced that not God but His acts change, or else the viewpoint from which man regards Him alters. The matter may not be so simple for the thinker who seeks to base his faith on a philosophical foundation; but the Torah is not a philosophical treatise, its sole purpose being to speak to the heart of man, and to implant faith therein.

If there are any here who still have doubts on the subject, and find it hard to imagine that in a unitary work divergent concepts of God like those mentioned should be conjointly reflected, I shall give them an example drawn from outside biblical literature. In the *Divina Commedia* of Dante Alighieri, next to the most spirited and colorful passages, full of wondrous tales that point every moment to the direct intervention of the Deity in human affairs, there are doctrinal passages, corresponding in their character and conception of God to the sections attributed to source P, just as the former passages bear comparison with the sections assigned to J and E. Nevertheless Dante was one, and his *Commedia* was one.

All that I have said so far concerns only a given portion of the aggregate of differences in the conception of the Deity to which I have drawn your attention in expounding the thesis of the documentary theory. There are still other divergences relating to the manner in which the theophany is experienced. In this regard we may ask the question: Does the view of the higher critics fit in with what we find in the text of the Bible? Let us go into the matter.

It is held, as I have stated, that there are three kinds of theophanies. Each one is characteristic of one of the sources: if God reveals Himself in corporeal form, the passage belongs to J; in dreams and visions by night, to E; in speech alone, to P.

Let us consider the divine manifestations in dream or vision. Prior to the time of Moses, there were seven instances of this type.

The first occurred when the Covenant of the Pieces was made (Gen. xv). What are we told there?—the following:

After these things the word of the Lord came to Abram IN A VISION, *saying*, etc. "The word of the Lord [YHWH]": since the name YHWH is mentioned here, the verse completely contradicts the view that visions are peculiar to source E, which uses *ʾElōhīm*. In order to extricate themselves from this perplexity, the critics delete the word *vision* on the basis of the very theory that itself requires proof. Gunkel, for instance, justifies the textual emendation on the ground that "theophanies in dream or vision are characteristic of E." This is an example of the kind of argument in a circle that I described to you yesterday.

The second occasion: the divine manifestation to Isaac. It is stated (xxvi 24): *And the Lord* [YHWH] *appeared to him the same night*. Here, too, we have the Tetragrammaton, which again conflicts with the theory mentioned above. In this case, the entire verse is omitted in order to remove the difficulty. The critical error is thus repeated.

The third instance: the theophany vouchsafed to Jacob in his famous dream, when he saw the ladder set upon the earth, with its top reaching to heaven. In this passage, likewise, YHWH occurs: *And behold, the Lord stood above it and said: 'I am the Lord* [YHWH],' etc. (xxviii 13); and also on this occasion the remedy is immediately to hand: the section is wholly dismembered, and the resultant pieces are re-formed into two parallel accounts, one containing the dream, and the other the manifestation of YHWH in corporeal form. The first narrative is assigned to E and the second to J.

If we do not tamper with the texts to force them to state the things we desire, and if we base our judgment on what is actually recorded in the Bible and not on what we write ourselves, or what we leave after our erasures and dissections, with a view to making the passages fit in with our preconceived ideas, we must come to the conclusion that out of these seven instances three are completely in conflict with the prevailing opinion.

And the remaining four? In two of them we are told about the dreams of Abimelech, king of Gerar, and of Laban the Aramean: *But God [ʾElōhīm] came to Abimelech in a dream by night, and said to him,* etc. (xx 3); so, too: *But God [ʾElōhīm] came to Laban the Aramean in a dream by night, and said to him,* etc. (xxxi 24). Here, as I explained two days ago, it was necessary to use the name *ʾElōhīm*, since Abimelech and Laban were strangers and did not know YHWH. Thus our texts provide no evidence of a specific source that uses the name *ʾElōhīm* instead of the Tetragrammaton, for every Hebrew author would have written *ʾElōhīm* in these circumstances.

Of the seven cases, then, only two remain. Even if no objection could be raised against them, these two examples could not prove anything against the first three, which are linked with the name YHWH. But they, too, are not free from difficulty. One of the theophanies occurs in Gen. xxxi 10-11: *In the mating season of the flock, I lifted up my eyes, and saw in a dream that the he-goats which leaped upon the flock were striped, spotted and mottled. Then the angel of* GOD *[ʾElōhīm] said to me in the dream, 'Jacob', and I said, 'Here I am!'* etc. Here, also, the name *ʾElōhīm* is used for a reason connected with the content of the story. It was not proper that YHWH Himself should appear to Jacob for the purpose of disclosing to him a matter of this nature. An angel sufficed; and even the angel is designated by Scripture "an angel of *ʾElōhīm*" and not "an angel of YHWH," in order to avoid associating in any way the most sacred name with such a theme.

The last theophany is that which was vouchsafed to Jacob when he was about to go down to Egypt: *And* GOD [*'Elōhīm*] *spoke to Israel in visions of the night, and said, 'Jacob, Jacob.' And he said: 'Here am I'* (xlvi 2). In this case, too, there is a special reason for the use of *'Elōhīm*. Not only in this passage but in all the sections appertaining to Egypt—those that relate the story of Joseph and his brethren, or describe how Jacob and his sons left Canaan, and how the children of Israel settled in Egypt and were enslaved there—the Tetragrammaton is never mentioned in any utterance, until YHWH Himself appears to Moses at Mount Horeb (Exod. iii). Not only when the speaker is an Egyptian, or is regarded as such, or when the words are addressed to an Egyptian, but even when Joseph soliloquizes, or when he speaks to his brothers and father after making himself known to them, or when the brothers talk among themselves, or when Jacob addresses Joseph or his sons, the name used is always *'Elōhīm*. After the Tetragrammaton has been mentioned a number of times in the story of Potiphar's wife (Gen. xxxix), in the objective narrative of the Torah but not in any utterance of the speakers (even there Joseph refers to *'Elōhīm*), the name YHWH does not appear at all in any of the concluding sections of the Book of Genesis, or in the beginning of the Book of Exodus, even in the impersonal statements of the Pentateuch, except once, in the Blessings of Jacob (xlix 18), which is a poem and consequently comes under the rule governing Hebrew poetry, as I explained in my lecture two days ago. The Tetragrammaton is, as it were, forgotten, and only *'Elōhīm* is used throughout these sections, as though the Torah wished to create the impression that when our ancestors lived in an alien country, far from the land that YHWH had chosen for his inheritance, their knowledge of YHWH was at a low ebb. They knew of God's existence in a general way, but the clear and complete knowledge of YHWH was lost to them, until YHWH revealed Himself in all His glory to Moses. For this reason Scripture tells us that when Jacob witnessed the theophany, it was *'Elōhīm* who revealed Himself to him, and said: *'I will go down with you to Egypt'* (Gen. xlvi 4). On going down to Egypt the children of Israel took with them the knowledge of *'Elōhīm*, but not the full knowledge of Yhwh. It was essential for a man like Moses to arise in order that the knowledge of *'Elōhīm* should be transformed again into the knowledge of Yhwh. This is what the Bible means when it states: *And 'Elōhīm spoke to Moses, and said unto him: 'I am Yhwh'* (Exod. vi 2). Thus we see that there was a definite reason for the use of the name *'Elōhīm* even in the account of Jacob's vision in Beer-sheba, and it does not represent the established usage of any particular source.[2]

Consequently, the entire conception that visions and dreams are the particular characteristic, as it were, of source E is no more than a figment of the imagination. A detailed study of the passages pertaining to the other theophanies would lead us, without difficulty, to the conclusion that the customary assertions regarding the theophanic features peculiar to J and P are likewise imaginary. But I do not wish to prolong the analysis, in order not to take up too much of your time with one subject, and I shall now go over to another topic. In any case, I have already said sufficient to demonstrate the weakness of the current view regarding the alleged differences, and to satisfy ourselves that whatever is stated on the strength of these divergences is unfounded.

It is customary to point out differences between the sources in yet another very important sphere, namely, that of ethics. In outline, the dominant view is as follows:

Although the sources J and E endeavor to present the patriarchs to us as ideal figures, and give us wonderful examples of their lofty morality, such as Abraham's faith and Joseph's righteousness, yet they do not refrain from including also a few episodes that are ethically open to objection, for instance, the story of how Jacob obtained the blessing of his aged father by deceit. This proves that the moral sense of J and E was defective, whereas the ethical understanding of P was alert and sensitive, and operated on a lofty plane that was beyond all reproach.

If we wish to test the correctness of this view and to ascertain whether the moral standards of certain sections differ from those of others, it is advisable that we should consider, in the first instance, the section that has become a particular target for criticism, to wit, the incident when, on the advice of his mother, Jacob went to take his father's benison by guile (Gen. xxvii). Jacob and Rebekah certainly committed a great sin; about that there is no doubt. But this is not the issue. The question is how the Torah judges the act, and what attitude it adopts thereto; it is this that determines the moral level of the narrative. Let us seek the answer in the biblical text.

It should be stated, by way of preface, that it is a fundamental principle of Scripture, in narratives of this nature, not to express its judgment explicitly and subjectively, but to relate the story in an objective manner, leaving it to the reader to learn the "moral" from the way the events unfold in accordance with the will of the Judge of the universe. Undoubtedly a lesson that is taught by implication is capable of exerting a greater influence than one explicitly stated.

Now what happened to Jacob after he had tricked his father and obtained by deception the blessing intended for his brother Esau? Not only was he compelled to go into exile, which is itself a punishment for the sin he had committed, but God also exacted retribution from him measure for measure. Jacob had exploited the darkness that covered his father's blind eyes in order to come before him in his brother's stead, and lo! after he had slaved hard for seven years, and was waiting for Laban to give him the beloved of his heart, Laban took advantage of the darkness of night to cheat him by substituting one sister for another in his chamber. One sister in place of another: exactly as he had entered Isaac's tent in place of his brother. The punishment is clear, nor is the verdict pronounced by the Torah on Jacob in doubt. Even the wording of Laban's retort to Jacob's complaint in the morning, IT IS NOT DONE SO *in our country to give the* YOUNGER BEFORE THE FIRST BORN (Gen. xxix 26), is calculated to recall to Jacob—and also to the reader—the bitter memory of what had happened to his father when the younger son was presented to him before the first born, for so it is not done!

What now of Rebekah? She, too, was punished with poetic justice. She had said to her son Jacob, when she counselled him to usurp the blessing: Now, THEREFORE, MY SON, OBEY MY VOICE *as I command you* (xxvii 8). Her retribution was that she was compelled to send this her dearly loved son away, to urge him to leave the country, and to tell him this in the very same words: NOW, THEREFORE, MY SON, OBEY MY VOICE (*v.* 43). The allusion is obvious. By the parallelism of phrasing the Torah brings the link between the two episodes into relief. The story is thus not only free from any moral taint, but on the contrary it inculcates a sublime moral lesson: Scripture teaches us that anyone acting in this way is destined to receive his punishment, severe retribution corresponding to his crime, be the sinner who he may—be it even Jacob, even Rebekah.

It would not have been unprofitable to examine also the other narratives of this kind, for example, the story of Abram and Sarai in Egypt (xii 10-20) and the parallel accounts (xx; xxvi 7-11); the episode of the sale of the birthright by Esau to Jacob (xxv 29-34); the tale of Jacob and Laban (especially xxx 25-43), and the like. But time presses, and I must be brief. Anyone who refers to my book, *La Questione*, will find there all the material in full. But the example I have cited is sufficient to show that if we are not content with a cursory and superficial glance at the subject, we must ultimately be convinced that the imaginary disparities wholly disappear when we scrutinize the biblical texts with a discerning eye.

Despite the lack of time, there is one question that merits our attention for a moment even at this stage. I can well understand that you may now argue: On the basis of what we have learnt today, explicitly or implicitly, we are ready to concede that there is no reason to find fault with the ethical standards of the narratives of J and E, and that on the contrary the attentive reader may derive from them noble ethical instruction; but why is there not a single passage in P that requires close examination in order to learn its moral? If J and E relate that the patriarchs sinned and were subsequently punished, why is P completely silent about their transgressions? Is there not a difference between one who sins and is punished and one who does not sin at all? Is this not a divergency that distinguishes the sources? The answer is simple and clear. Not a single section containing narratives about the activities of the patriarchs is assigned to P, except the story of the Cave of Machpelah and the section of the Circumcision. To this source are ascribed dry and fragmentary reports, genealogical and chronological data, and little else. Since in general hardly any narratives are assigned to this document, it is impossible to find there, apart from the two solitary instances mentioned, stories of any kind. Just as narratives of the type referred to are wanting, so there are also lacking didactic tales like those that exemplify the faith of Abraham and the virtue of Joseph.

Let us pass on to another subject—the differences in family and communal customs. In this instance, too, we shall choose one of the most typical examples, one that is also considered among the most conclusive. It is usually stated—and every scholar repeats the assertions of his predecessors without thinking of investigating the matter in the least—that in source P it is the father who names the newborn son, whereas in J and E it is the mother who gives the name; this indicates that the documents emanated from different environments where different customs prevailed. P originated in a place and time that gave the right to name the child to the father, whilst the other sources were written in a place and time that bestowed this privilege on the mother.

When we examine the sections ascribed to J and E, we see at once that *in most cases*, it is true, the name is given by the mother; nevertheless there is a considerable number of exceptions to this rule—fourteen exceptions to nineteen or twenty examples that conform to the rule. The number of exceptions is itself enough to arouse doubts; and if we bear in mind that all the instances connected with the children of Jacob constitute, in the final analysis, only one instance, since they are all found in a single section, the preponderating majority passes to the other side. As for the cases referred to P, that is to say, cases where the father of the son gives the name, their total does not exceed four; and even if they were free from all objection, it would be difficult to assign great importance to a rule built on such a small number of passages. But there are, in truth, objections—in ample measure. Two of these four cases have been attributed to P for the very reason that in them the father names the child—that is, on the basis of what these passages ought to prove, and hence, needless to say, prove nothing. In the third instance, it is doubtful if it is actually the father who names the son, and therefore this case also provides no evidence. Thus only one example is left, which is numerically nugatory. There is no difference, therefore, of sources here or variations of custom. The significance of the divergence has to be sought elsewhere.

If we study the passages carefully, we shall find the reason: it is clear and natural. When the Torah informs us of the name given to any child at birth, mostly it advances, as we know, an etymological explanation alluding to some circumstance that preceded or accompanied the birth. Now whenever this factor, to which the name owes its origin, is connected with the father, then the

naming of the child is ascribed to the father, and when it is related to the mother, then she is said to name the child. This rule
is simple and logical, and is valid in every case, without exception. When the circumstance appertains to the son himself or no
etymological explanation is offered (which rarely obtains), then
the rule does not, of course, apply; in one of these instances the
naming is ascribed to the father, in another to the mother, and in
the rest it is stated indefinitely, "one named" or "they named."

But perhaps, it will be argued, what all the various disparities
cannot prove, the openly conflicting passages may prove. Let us
test this; let us examine the text.

The most serious discrepancy in the entire Book of Genesis is
the difference between the two records of the names of the three
wives of Esau. In the section dealing with the "history" of Isaac
(xxvi 34, xxviii 9) it is stated that Esau took to wife Judith the
daughter of Beeri the Hittite, Basemath the daughter of Elon the
Hittite, and Mahalath the daughter of Ishmael, Abraham's son;
whereas according to the "history" of Esau (xxxvi 2-3), his wives
were: Adah daughter of Elon the Hittite, Oholibamah the daughter of Anah, the daughter of Zibeon the Hivite, and Basemath
Ishmael's daughter. This is an explicit inconsistency that cannot
possibly be reconciled; all the efforts of the harmonizers to do so
have failed. There are many other passages in Genesis that contradict
one another, or appear to do so, but the majority of them form
part of the duplicate narratives, which constitute a special subject
of study, and on which I propose to speak tomorrow. As for the
minority of these conflicting texts, which contain discrepancies
between isolated data (such as the names of Esau's wives), they
need not be detailed here, since my observations on the present
case are equally valid for the other disparities of this kind.

At first blush, it would seem that the documentary hypothesis
enables us to explain all these incongruities without the least difficulty: one of the discrepant passages emanates from one source,

the other from another source. But in truth this explanation fails to explain anything; for by exculpating the author from the responsibility for the contradiction and putting the blame on the redactor, we gain nothing. We have merely shifted the problem from one place to another without solving it. An editor who does his work conscientiously is obliged to avoid inconsistencies no less than the author, possibly even more so. Nor is it feasible to maintain that the redactor was aware of the disparity but did not dare to tamper with the sources, for on other occasions we are told repeatedly that he erased or omitted or altered or added exactly as he was minded. Furthermore, it is inconceivable that just in the case of Esau's wives the editor adopted an attitude of meticulous respect for the source, since according to the generally accepted view with regard to the distribution of the sources, both the list of Esau's wives given in the section of Isaac's "history" and the whole of Esau's "history" are attributed to P; thus the higher critics are compelled to assume that the redactor expunged from Esau's history what he found in P and substituted for it data from another source. If so, the editor purposely introduced this inconsistency into his compilation. What was his object in doing so? The question, therefore, returns to its starting point. The problem of the contradictions cannot be solved by the documentary hypothesis.

Can we find a solution without its help? I think we can. It appears that there were current among the Israelites in regard to the names of Esau's wives, and likewise with reference to the other topics that similarly recur in contradictory versions, two divergent traditions; but the Torah did not wish to reject one in favor of the other, and therefore found room for both in its text, leaving it to the reader to choose one of the versions or to find a way of reconciling them as he deemed fit. In Talmudic literature such instances are legion.

It is thus seen that what the discrepancies—mentioned first— were unable to prove, the inconsistencies cannot prove either.

To conclude: we have probed the third pillar in its most vital parts, and we have seen that its material is no more solid than that of the previous two pillars. The third pillar has also failed to stand the test.

DUPLICATIONS AND REPETITIONS

THE FOURTH PILLAR is founded on the existence of duplications and repetitions.[1] Anyone who reads the Book of Genesis cannot fail to notice that many stories occur twice, and a few even three times. Upon closer study he will also see that the duplications and triplications are of two kinds. Sometimes the parallel sections appertain—or are considered to do so—entirely to one subject, which is depicted in each of them in a different form and with variation of detail. Such, for instance (it is the classic example that is constantly quoted), are the first section of the Book of Genesis—the story of the creation of the world—and the beginning of the second section—on the Garden of Eden—which is also regarded as a second account of the story of Creation. These examples may be termed "Duplications." At other times, the parallel sections are concerned with events that are unrelated to each other but yet are so similar in their principal motifs that one may conjecture that they are simply divergent developments of a single narrative. Such passages, in which the Bible reverts to given themes on different occasions, may be called "Repetitions." The classic instance of repetition—it is usually the first to be quoted—is that of the narratives that describe the experiences of the matriarchs in the palaces of foreign kings: Sarah in Egypt (Gen. xii 10-20); Sarah, again, in Gerar (ch. xx); Rebekah, likewise in Gerar (xxvi 7-11). The occurrence of duplications and repetitions is considered to be one of the most conclusive proofs in favor of the ruling documentary theory. It is held to demonstrate clearly that the redactor had before him various sources that told the same story in different ways, or presented different versions of an ancient tradition; he accordingly extracted from each of them what he found ready to hand and incorporated the whole material into his compilation, without concerning himself with the fact that in doing so he was repeating one theme two or three times, or was recapitulating a single event in two or three conflicting forms.

This is the current view. We must now test its validity. In accordance with my practice in the preceding lectures, I shall not detain you with observations of a general nature, for they are not very helpful in clarifying the subject, since every generalization can be met by a counter-generalization. More important is the concrete investigation of the text. Hence I shall not mention the general objections raised against the above-mentioned interpretation of the occurrence of parallel sections, nor shall I deal with the observations made in this regard by other scholars. I shall not spend time on this, but I shall proceed at once to examine the passages.

As I wish to keep my remarks within the bounds of a single lecture, I shall have to content myself today, too, with examples only. I think it will be best to select precisely those classic instances that I have mentioned, to wit, the duplication of the story of Creation and the repetition of the incidents that befell the matriarchs. Although even in relation to these examples lack of time will not permit us to say all that could be said on the matter, yet I hope that we shall succeed in elucidating the core of the problem adequately.

Let us begin with the story of Creation. The first section of the Torah, from *In the beginning God created* (i 1) to *which He had creatively made* (ii 3), describes, as we know, the creation of the whole universe in all its parts in six days, and the exalted character of the seventh day, on which God abstained from His work and took pleasure in the world that He had made. This is followed by the story of the Garden of Eden, which tells us again, in the first portion, about the creation of Adam and his wife, and which modern scholars regard as another account of Creation, a kind of second cosmogony, differing from the first. The first account, which uses the name אֱלֹהִים *Elōhīm*, is ascribed to P, and the second, which employs ה׳ אֱלֹהִים YHWH *Elōhīm*, is assigned to J. On this there is complete unanimity. The critics disagree only in regard to the internal composition of each of the two sections; but we shall not discuss this dispute now, since it is not germane to our subject.

It is manifest that the two sections differ considerably in character. About this there can be no doubt. The divergence is obvious if we approach the text without bias. In the first section we are vouchsafed a sublime vision of the totality of creation, portrayed with great synthetic power, which unifies into a clear and comprehensible order all the endlessly changing categories of existence; we perceive there, enthroned on high, the Idea that rises above the accidental, the temporal and the finite, and depicts for us with complete simplicity of expression the vast expanses of the universe to their utmost limits. God reveals Himself—a point with which we have already dealt—as a transcendental being dwelling in His supernal abode without direct contact with the creatures. On the other hand, the second section contains a graphic and dramatic narrative that captivates the heart with its details imbued as they are with the magic hues of the oriental imagination, and seeks to inculcate religious and ethical teachings under the guise of actual happenings, addressing itself more to the feelings than to the intellect of the reader. YHWH appears there, as we have already noted, in direct touch with His creature man and with the other created beings of His world. The difference, therefore, is profound from several aspects, and only one who closed his eyes to the obvious could deny it. Nevertheless, this does not prove the mechanical amalgamation by a later editor of two passages derived from two different documents.

When the Torah was written, there already existed among the Israelites a number of traditions concerning the creation of the world and the beginning of human life upon earth. All the ancient peoples of the Orient made this important topic the theme of numerous sagas reflecting their beliefs and concepts, and it is inconceivable that in the early generations of our people, too, the fathers did not recount stories on this subject to their children, and teachers to their pupils. There were undoubtedly all kinds of traditions: on the one hand, the narratives handed down in the circles of the sages and philosophers, who devoted profound study to the mystery of the world's origin; and on the other, the folk tales that circulated among the broad masses of the people, stories that were understood by all and that were suited to explain abstruse matters to the simple mind of a humble shepherd, stories that were colorful and vivid, and were able to speak to a man's heart. Needless to say, when the Torah came to give an account of the genesis of man and the world, it did not ignore these traditions. It was but natural that the Torah should take up an attitude towards them; that it should teach us how to extract their kernel and to throw away the husk, how to interpret them and how to distill from them whatever is good and true, how to purify them so that they should conform to the religious conscience of the Israelites, and how to profit by them for generations to come. And so the Torah did. When we compare its inaugural sections with what we learn about the ancient traditions from the non-Israelite documents, from the allusions to them in biblical prophecy and poetry, and from the legends that were preserved by the Jewish people and were incorporated in the Midrashim of the rabbinic sages, it becomes clear that these traditions served the Torah as raw material for its own structure. It selected from them what was suitable; it purified and refined their content; it removed therefrom what was left of, or what had seeped in from, the pagan beliefs that were incongruous with its teachings, and conversely, it emphasized whatever was useful to its educational aims. Both of the aforementioned types of traditions—the traditions of the circles of the "Sages" and those accepted by the general populace—served the Bible's purpose simultaneously. The former did so in the first section, which comes to teach us that the heavens and the earth were created by the fiat of the One God, and not as a result of the quarrels of the gods who, as the pagan peoples related, waged war against one another, or in consequence of the heroic deeds of YHWH against the rebellious forces of nature, as the poets of Israel used to tell; but that everything came into being by His word, for His will is not subject to any form of opposition, and He is not compelled to set aside the desire of others for the sake of His. The traditions of the second category were used by the Torah in the second section, in which it aimed to make the early history of Adam and Eve a source of moral instruction, for the experiences of the fathers are a sign to the children and inculcate the duties that devolve upon us in our religious and ethical life. Consequently, we should not be surprised at the fact that in the first section the characteristics of the wisdom tradition are still reflected, and that in the second we can still detect features of the traditions current among the multitude. All the disparities between the two sections that we have mentioned are entirely explicable on the basis of this theory.

Possibly the question may be raised at this juncture: But, apart from the general differences, the details of the narrative in the first section are inconsistent with those of the second; how then is it possible to regard them as forming a unitary composition, since they conflict with each other in their content? The higher critics have already drawn attention to a number of points of contradiction or antithesis between them. We must accordingly examine the passages in order to ascertain the nature and value of these differences. There are five points; let us consider them seriatim.

Point one. In contradistinction to the six days mentioned in the first section, it is stated at the beginning of the second (ii 4): IN THE DAY *that the Lord God made the earth and the heavens*; this indicates that the earth and the heavens were created in one day. However, there is no need for lengthy argument to show that in truth there is no discrepancy here at all. Anyone who is not insensitive to Hebrew usage realizes at once that the expression "In the day that the Lord God made" means simply "At the time that He made," and does not refer to a "day" of twelve or twenty-four hours. It is written, for example, IN THE DAY *when the Lord spoke with Moses on Mount Sinai* (Num. iii 1), although the colloquy lasted forty days and forty nights. We also find: ON THE DAY *when the Lord delivered him from the hand of all his enemies, and from the hand of Saul* (Psalms xviii 1; the wording in ii Sam. xxii 1 is almost identical), although, needless to say, David was not delivered from the hand of *all* his enemies in one day. So, too, we are accustomed in modern Hebrew to say "in the hour that," which does not mean an hour of sixty minutes but merely "when."

The second point is no more difficult than the first. According to the first section, Creation began with the waters of the deep, the waters of the primordial ocean (Gen. i 2); but, it is asserted, from the opening verses of the second section (ii 5f.) it appears, on the contrary, that Creation was inaugurated with the dry land. This objection, however, is valid only if we disturb the unity of the text and regard the two narratives as independent accounts, in other words, if we consider as already proven what still remains to be proved. If, in truth, the combined sections form a continuous whole, it is clear that from the standpoint of the second section, too, Creation commenced with the waters of the deep, which are mentioned at the beginning.

The third problem is also not unduly difficult. A discrepancy is pointed out between the statement in the first section, *male and female He created them* (i 27), that is to say, that they were both created together, and the story of the Garden of Eden, according to which the man was formed first (ii 7) and then the woman (ii 21-22). This is also not a real difficulty. To begin with, when man is referred to as one creature among many—be he even the highest of them—and his genesis is mentioned only as a link in the great chain of creative acts, the manner of his creation is described, of course, only in general terms, in the simple phrase, *male and female He created them*; but we are not told *how* they were made. It is written neither that they were created at the same time, nor that they were formed one after the other; we have only the indefinite statement that they were created. Afterwards, when the Bible comes to elaborate the story of mankind's origin, it explains in detail *how* man and woman were formed respectively. This is a case not of inconsistency, but of a general statement followed by a detailed account, which is a customary literary device of the Torah.

Two points remain, which are, indeed, real difficulties, and on which we shall have to dwell at some length.

The fourth disparity is as follows: we are told in the first section that the plants were formed on the third day and man on the sixth, whereas in the second section we read that until the creation of man *no* שִׂיחַ *śīaḥ of the field were yet in the earth and no* עֵשֶׂב *'ēsebh of the field had yet sprung up* (ii 5); furthermore, that after man had been made, *the Lord God made to grow out of the ground every tree that is pleasant to the sight and good for food* (ii 9). A difficult problem to be sure; but only at the first blush!

It may well be that the ancient traditions that furnished the pentateuchal narratives with their material contradicted each other,
and that in one the vegetation came first, and in the other, man;
it is also possible that some traces of this original discrepancy are
still discernible in the Torah's expression. This is feasible, but it
does not affect the issue. The question confronting us is: Is there a
contradiction in the Torah itself? Let us first note that the plants
mentioned as missing at the time of man's creation are only "*śiaḥ*
of the field" and "*ēsebh* of the field," and these do not constitute
all plant life. It is true that the commentators who search for inconsistencies usually enlarge the signification of these expressions;
Dillmann, for instance, writes: "shrubs [*śiaḥ*] and herbs [*ēsebh*] are
specified here as the most important (*sic!*) categories of the vegetable world, and are representative thereof." But whoever examines
the matter without pre-conceived ideas will not readily agree to
the view that "*śiaḥ*" of the field" and "*ēsebh* of the field" are the
most important species of the vegetable kingdom and its chief rep-
resentatives. If Scripture tells us that just these plants had not yet
grown, it is these kinds and no others that are intended. On the
contrary, the negation also implies an affirmation, to wit, that the
other plants were already to be found on the earth. What then is
the significance of the absence of these particular species? Let us
turn to the end of the passage. It is subsequently stated, at the
conclusion of the story of the Garden of Eden: *thorns and thistles
it shall bring forth to you; and you shall eat the* ʿēsebh *of the field*
(iii 18); "*ēsebh* of the field"—the identical expression found in the
opening of the section; "thorns and thistles" are synonymous with
"*śiaḥ* of the field" mentioned at the beginning. Now we begin to
understand: there is a link between the commencement and the
end of the section. Those species were missing at first that were
later created in consequence of man's transgression: "*śiaḥ* of the
field," that is, "thorns and thistles," as a punishment, and "ʿ*ēsebh*

of the field," that is, wheat and barley and the like that were required for human sustenance, since man could no longer live on
the fruit of the Garden from which he had been banished.

Perhaps it may still be objected: But were not *all* the various
kinds of plants created on the third day, including these species?
This difficulty, however, can also be explained. In the first section it is written: *And God said, 'Let the earth put forth vegetation,
plants* YIELDING SEED, *and fruit trees bearing fruit each according to
its kind, in which is their* SEED, *upon the earth.' And it was so. And
the earth brought forth vegetation, plants* YIELDING SEED *according to
their own kinds, and trees bearing fruit in which is there* SEED, *each
according to its kind* (i 11-12). It appears strange, at first glance,
that the Torah stresses here repeatedly the idea of "seed" and the
"yielding of seed." Nor is this all; further on, too, in the words
God addresses to man, it is similarly stated: *Behold, I have given
you every plant* YIELDING SEED *which is upon the face of all the
earth, and every tree with* SEED *in its fruit; you shall have them for
food* (i 29). Such emphasis, reiterated so often, undoubtedly has a
purpose. It is none other than this: to show clearly that there is
no discrepancy whatsoever between what is stated here and what
would later be written in the second section. The plants that are
created on the third day are those that are capable of reproducing
themselves afterwards by means of seed. This excludes those for
which seed alone is not sufficient; they need something else in addition, something that had not yet come into the world. We are
specifically told in connection with the "*śiaḥ* of the field" and the
"*ʿēsebh* of the field": *Now no śiaḥ of the field were yet in the earth
and no ēśebh of the field had yet sprung up, for the Lord God had
not caused it to rain upon the earth,* AND THERE WAS NO MAN TO
TILL THE GROUND. There was no "*śiaḥ* of the field" because the
Lord God had not yet *caused it to rain* upon the earth, and "*ʿēsebh*
of the field" had not yet sprung up because *there was no man* to

till the ground. Every year we see in summer that, although the
seeds of the thorns and thistles lie scattered on the ground in
large numbers, not one of them springs up; but no sooner does
rain fall than the earth becomes covered with thorns and thistles.
As for the "*ēsebh* of the field," even though isolated specimens of
wheat and barley and the like do exist in a natural state, yet they
are not found in great quantities in one place; fields of grain are
produced only by man.

With regard to the statement a few verses lower down: *And the
Lord God made to grow out of the ground every tree that is pleasant
to the sight and good for food*, etc. (*v.* 9), these words must not be
interpreted apart from their context. Earlier it is written: *And the
Lord God planted a garden in Eden, in the east* (*v.* 8); and here it is
explained how they were planted—a general statement followed by
a detailed description. What does the gardener do when he plants
a new garden? Although he produces new trees from the soil, he
does not create new *species*. Even so the Lord God did: in order
to make the garden He caused good trees to grow out of its soil,
of the species that He had already created on the third day.

The fifth point is of a similar nature; hence we can deal with
it briefly. We find in the second section that the Lord God formed
out of the ground the beasts and the flying creatures (*v.* 19);
whereas the first section informs us that the beasts and the flying creatures were created before man. But in this case, too, we
have to be careful not to regard the words of the Bible as though
they were isolated and unrelated to their context. According to the
continuation of the passage, the Lord God's intention was to pass
in review before the man all the species of animals in order that
he should give them names, and endeavor to find among them a
helper corresponding to him. The cattle, which should have been
the first to be considered in this connection, are not mentioned
at all among the kinds of animals that the Lord God then made.
Yet we are explicitly told afterwards that Adam gave names to the

cattle, the beasts and the flying creatures (*v.* 20). This implies that the cattle, owing to their nature, were already to be found in the garden with man, in agreement with the first section. But in order that all the various kinds of beasts and flying creatures that were scattered through the length and breadth of the world should also be represented in Adam's abode, the Lord God formed, from the soil of the garden, beasts and flying creatures of every type previously created, and He brought them to the man.

In general this second section, in its present form, contains no cosmological description of any kind. Not only is there no reference in it to the hosts of heaven, or to the sea and the fish—several scholars have already noted this fact—but even the creation of heaven and earth is mentioned only incidentally, whilst the creation of the domestic animals is completely omitted, and of the entire vegetable kingdom we find only the trees of the Garden of Eden and the species connected with man's sin; of the beasts and the flying creatures reference is made only to those that were brought before Adam so that he might name them. What we have before us here then is simply a detailed description of the creation of man, which had been alluded to in general terms in the preceding section, in accordance with the literary method that requires first a general statement and thereafter a detailed account—an expedient that, as we stated earlier, is very frequently employed in the Torah.

It follows from all that we have observed thus far that there is no disparity between the two sections, and there is nothing to show that they were not connected at the time of their composition. On the contrary, indications of a link between them came to light almost of their own accord as soon as we started to delve into them more deeply, and we shall succeed in finding further signs of this nexus when we study their content in detail. For example, unmistakable evidence of a close connection becomes apparent when we consider the answer that the Torah gives to the vexed question of the existence of evil in the world: how is it possible that in the world of the Almighty, the good and beneficent God, there should be so much suffering and calamity and all the different evils that befall us? The solution offered to us in the two sections treated as one is as follows: the world itself, as it left the hand of the Creator, is very good (i 31), but man's transgressions are the cause of all kinds of evil (iii 16-19). When we study the two sections as a continuous whole, we receive this answer: but once we separate them, we learn from each one only half the answer.

But it is time for us to pass on to the problem of the repetitions, and to examine the classic example in this field, namely, the three stories that I have mentioned concerning the matriarchs. According to the current view, the first emanated from a given stratum of J, the second from source E, and the third from another stratum of J. Let us proceed to investigate the subject.

When we glance at the first narrative, which refers to the episode of Abram and Sarai in Egypt (xii 10-20), we are immediately made aware of a remarkable parallel between what is related there and what we are told subsequently regarding the children of Israel when they went down to Egypt. There is hardly a verse or half a verse in this passage that does not remind us of a parallel in connection with the children of Israel. This is true not only of these expressions that were already noted by the rabbinic sages for homiletical purposes (Bereshith Rabba xl 8), but of all the details of the entire section, down to the smallest minutiae. Here, in the first verse, it is stated: *Now there was a famine in the land... for the famine was severe in the land*; and there: *Now the famine was severe in the land* (xliii 1), and again: *for the famine is severe in the land of Canaan* (xlvii 4). In our passage, still in the same verse, we are informed that Abram went down to Egypt to sojourn there, and later on we are told that Joseph's brothers said to Pharaoh: We have come to *sojourn* in the land (xlvii 4).

Abram's anxiety lest the Egyptians kill him and let his wife live (*vv.* 11-13, especially *v.* 12: *then they will kill me, but they will let you live*) recalls the decrees of Pharaoh recorded in the Book of Exodus: *if it is a son, you shall kill him; but if it is a daughter, she shall live* (Exod. i 16), and thereafter: *Every son that is born you shall cast into the Nile, but you shall let every daughter live* (*v.* 22). The statement here concerning the taking of Sarai into the palace of the king of Egypt to be one of his handmaids (Gen. xii 14-15) parallels the account there of how the children of Israel likewise were taken as slaves unto Pharaoh. In our narrative, reference is made to the presents that were given to Abram (*v.* 16: *and for her sake he dealt well with Abram*, etc.) and to the fact that Abram, when he went up from Egypt, *was very rich in cattle,* IN SILVER, AND IN GOLD (xiii 2); and in the Exodus story, mention is made of *jewelry of silver and of gold* and of clothing that the children of Israel received from the Egyptians when they went forth. In both passages the Torah tells us that the Lord heard the cry of the oppressed and smote Pharaoh with *plagues* in order that he should let them go free (the word *plague* occurs here in xii 17, and in Exod. xi 1). The first stage of the liberation is described in like terms in both cases. Here it is stated: *So Pharaoh called Abram, and said* (Gen. xii 18), and there: *And he summoned Moses and Aaron by night, and said* (Exod. xii 31). In our story, Pharaoh says to Abram: *take (her) and be gone* [the verbs are singular] (Gen. xii 19); and in the account of the Exodus, Pharaoh says to Moses and Aaron: TAKE... *as you have said,* AND BE GONE (Exod. xii 32; in the Septuagint exactly as in our passage, *take and be gone* [only the verbs are plural]). Furthermore, our text reads: AND THEY SET *him* ON THE WAY [*wayešalleḥū*, literally, "And they sent away, let go"] *with his wife and all that he had,* using the very verb *šillaḥ* ["let go"] that recurs so often in the Book of Exodus in relation to the children of Israel. After leaving Egypt, Abram *went up to the Negeb* (Gen. xiii 1), just as the spies, whom

Moses sent to spy out the land after the departure of the children of Israel from Egypt, went up to the Negeb (Num. xiii 17: *Go up into the Negeb yonder*; *v.* 22: *They went up into the Negeb*). In the same way as it is written here of Abram: *And he went on his journeys* (Gen. xiii 3), so it is said of the children of Israel: *All the congregation of the people of Israel journeyed...* BY STAGES [literally, "their journeys"] (Exod. xvii 1); and similar expressions are to be found in many other parts of the Pentateuch (Exod. xl 36, 38; Num. x 6, 12; xxxiii 1, 2). Finally, our narrative records that Abram reached the place of the altar, which he had built at first *between Bethel and Ai*, the very place where his descendants were destined to fight their first battle for the conquest of the land on the western side of the Jordan.

Clearly, this is no mere coincidence. Without doubt, the Torah underscored these parallels intentionally. In order to understand the Torah's purpose, we must also pay attention to the parallelism between the preceding narrative (Gen. xii 1-9), which tells how Abram went up to the land of Canaan, and the later story that describes how his descendants entered the country. Abram came up from the North, and traversed the whole land of Canaan in three stages. The first journey brought him to *Shechem*, where he built an altar unto the Lord, a symbol, as it were, of the ideal conquest of the land in the name of the Lord (*vv.* 6-7). On the second journey, he reached a place east of Bethel, where he pitched his tent, *having Bethel on the west and Ai on the east*; and again he built there an altar unto the Lord, a further symbol of the conquest of the land in the name of his God (*v.* 8). On the third lap he journeyed on, still going toward the *Negeb* (*v.* 9), and at *Hebron* he acquired the field of Machpelah and the cave therein (xxiii 17-20).

Similar to these were the journeys of Jacob when he returned from Paddan-aram. Jacob entered Canaan from the northeast, came as far as *Shechem*, bought the piece of land where he pitched his tent at the full price, and erected there an altar to "El-Elohe-Israel" ["God, the God of Israel"] (xxxiii 18-20). There he remained until his sons captured the city of Shechem (xxxiv 25-29); and before he departed from there, he commanded all his household and all who were with him, with a view to their preparation for the journey up to Bethel: *Put away the foreign gods that are among you* (xxxv 2); and the images of the gods that he received from them he hid *under the oak which was near Shechem* (*v.* 4).

Thereafter he proceeded as far as Bethel, and at Bethel he, too, built an altar unto his God. Finally, he continued his journey toward the *Negeb*, and reached *Hebron* (xxxv 27).

Now the principal milestones in the journeys of Abram and Jacob present a remarkable parallel to those of the conquest of the land, in the days of Joshua. The first city to be seized by force of arms was *Ai... east of Bethel* (Jos. vii 2), and the children of Israel, who were making ready to capture it, were stationed *between Bethel and Ai, to the west of Ai* (viii 9; compare *v.* 12). The Book of Joshua also relates, immediately after the story of the conquest of Ai, that Joshua built an altar unto the Lord on Mount Ebal, that is, *next to* SHECHEM (viii 30); this means that he had gained control of the central portion of the land, between *Ai-Bethel* to the south and *Shechem* to the north, which corresponds to the middle stage of the journeys of Abram and Jacob. From there the children of Israel spread to the two remaining areas, to the south of *Ai-Bethel* (ch. x), and to the north of *Shechem* (ch. xi). It is the identical tripartite division of the land that we have already seen in the case of Abram and Jacob. In *Shechem* Joshua commanded the children of Israel: *Put away the foreign gods which are among you* (xxiv 23), using the very words that Jacob had once employed. There he made a covenant with the people that day, and he took a great stone and set it up there *under the oak* that was in the sanctuary of the Lord (*vv.* 25-26).

All these parallels are certainly not coincidental. The reiteration of the expressions that had previously been used in the narratives of Abram and Jacob prove conclusively that they are cited with special intent. The purpose is undoubtedly to teach us that the acts of the fathers are a sign unto the children; that the conquest of the land had, as it were, already taken place symbolically in the time of the patriarchs; that the patriarchs had also been privileged to lay the primary foundations of the real conquest through the acquisition of pieces of ground by purchase, and through the capture of the city of Shechem with their sword and bow; furthermore, and supremely, that this betokens an implicit promise made by the Lord to the patriarchs, which subsequently received complete fulfillment in the actual subjugation of the land by their descendants.

The same applies to the story of Abram and Sarai in Egypt and the parallel it provides to the fate of the children of Israel. Here, too, the history of the fathers foreshadows the destiny of the children. This episode, likewise, contains an implicit promise that was given to Abram and Sarai and was realized in their offspring. Also in this story the moral is inculcated that the word of the Lord endures forever, and that just as His help was granted to Abram and his wife and was renewed unto their children when they were similarly situated, so it is destined to be vouchsafed once more to their descendants in every period, whenever they should need it—a doctrine that was to serve as a source of comfort and hope throughout the generations.

Now that we have grasped the underlying meaning of this narrative, we can understand the significance of the cognate stories and explain why the three of them follow one another. At the time when the Torah was written, there were current among the Israelites a number of traditions concerning the patriarchs, just as there were sagas about the work of creation; and the Torah chose from among them those that were able to advance its purpose.

Three similar tales were in existence: one with regard to Abram's wife in Egypt, another about her in Gerar, and one concerning Isaac's wife in Gerar. It is possible that all three flowed from one ancient saga, but this belongs to the pre-history of the subject and has no bearing on our problem. We are interested only in the fact that if the acceptance of the three stories harmonized with and promoted the Torah's aim, there was no reason to exclude them. So, too, the Roman historian Livy, when he found two similar accounts about the two heroes, Decius Mus—father and son—who gave their lives on the field of battle as an offering to their god, in order to ensure victory for the Roman armies, he did not hesitate to include both of them in his book, despite the similarity of the episode of the father to that of the son. This in no way affects the unity of Livy's work. In our case, the reason that induced the Torah to accept the three existing traditions was the concept that everything that is done twice and thrice is to be regarded as confirmed and established. Even the symbolic conquest of the land that was first carried out by Abram was repeated in the case of Jacob, until it was completely realized in the days of Joshua. Similarly the teaching and promise contained for Israel in the first story of Sarai's stay with Pharaoh was corroborated and confirmed by the second episode in connection with Abimelech, and was strengthened and consolidated by the narrative of Rebekah, until they were fulfilled in their descendants and remained valid for endless generations. This method of recapitulation for the purpose of validation stems from the Semitic practice of using parallelism in order to give emphasis and prominence to an idea. In connection with the pentateuchal narratives, the significance of these repetitions is distinctly referred to in Joseph's statement to Pharaoh, when he interpreted his dream: *And the doubling of Pharaoh's dream means that the thing is fixed by God, and God will shortly bring it to pass* (Gen. xli 32). The Torah itself tells us here explicitly what the reiterations signify, and testifies that it is accustomed to repeat its teachings when it desires to inform us that a matter is established by God and that He will shortly bring it to pass.

This is a case, then, of intentional recapitulation, and not something that happened by chance in the course of the work of some later redactor.

I believe that the examples we have given above provide sufficient proof that the subject of today's discourse also does not support the documentary hypothesis, and that the fourth pillar likewise begins to crumble when we attempt to put to actual test the material of which it is constructed.

THE COMPOSITE SECTIONS

THERE IS STILL ONE PILLAR left for us to probe: the "Composite Sections."[1] To this test we shall devote our lecture today.

In the same way as there are parallels between one section and another, so we find in many sections internal parallels between one verse and another. Most critics regard these parallels as superfluous duplications or as manifest contradictions, which can be explained only on the basis of the hypothesis that each of these sections was pieced together from different elements, that is to say, that it was formed by combining verses or fragments of verses culled from two or three original sections all belonging to one theme. This is how, it is imagined, the editor set about his task: he took two narratives, one, for instance, from source J, and the other from E, both dealing with the same subject; he began to copy a few words or a complete sentence or several sentences from the first account, and then he proceeded to copy a few words or a complete verse or several verses from the second; later he left the second document and continued to copy from the first, returning subsequently to the second, and so on until all the material at his disposal was used up, and both stories had been welded into a single narrative.

Sometimes there were three accounts available to him, in which case he would also incorporate into his compilation, here and there, material from the third source. On occasion he would interpolate something of his own—explanations or connecting phrases or general notes. Apart from all this, we sometimes observe even in the original sources themselves signs of internal synthesis, the combination of materials derived from different strata and linked together by the particular editor of that document.

In order to test the correctness of this theory, it seems to me that it will be essential in this instance, even more than in the case of the previous matters that we discussed, to rely solely on an examination of the biblical text, without entering into general considerations. Hence, I shall not dwell on the questions with which other scholars have already dealt at length, for example, whether the description given above of the way the redactor did his work appears feasible or not, and similar issues. It is better to turn at once to Scripture and seek the answer there.

The nature of the subject with which we shall be occupied today requires that we should not collect the material for discussion from various passages, but that we should concentrate our study on one in particular, so that we may investigate it with due thoroughness. We shall have to consider subtle problems concerned with the logical and grammatical relationship between verses and half-verses, and the internal construction of sections; it will be more advantageous, therefore, for us to conduct our examination in depth rather than in breadth. Let us choose a particularly characteristic section from among those that are regarded as composite, and let us investigate it in detail.

Especially worthy of consideration in this respect is the section narrating the story of the blessing that Isaac bestowed on Jacob (Gen. xxvii), with which we have already dealt from another viewpoint in one of the previous lectures. The analysis of its sources is held to be one of the most valid achievements of the documentary hypothesis, and therefore the study of its internal composition is particularly important for the elucidation of the character and value of these textual divisions.

It is accepted by the majority of exegetes that the sources from which the verses of this section derive are J on one side and E on the other. They may differ as to which verses or parts of verses should be assigned to J and which to E, but in general they are agreed that the section is a tapestry woven by the redactor from elements extracted from these two documents. With a fine and penetrating analytical technique, these scholars have sought to retrace the entire course of the editor's work, to dissect the section into its original parts, to separate the two types of text according to their sources, and to rebuild from these fragmentary passages the two original narratives that the redactor used. In particular Hermann Gunkel, in his commentary on Genesis, excelled in this research. Verses 15 and 16, which describe how Jacob disguised himself in order to enter his father's presence in his brother's stead, served as the starting point of his analysis. According to the first verse, Jacob put on his brother's garments; according to the second verse, he covered his hands and the smooth part of his neck with skins of kids. Gunkel's theory postulates that each of these two parallel devices—the garments of Esau and the skins of the kids—belongs to a different source; on this basis he subdivides the entire section. Every verse or fragment of a verse that mentions Esau's clothes, and every verse or part of a verse that is linked—or so it appears to him—to a verse in which reference is made to Esau's attire, he ascribes to one source; conversely, whatever has a bearing, directly or indirectly, on the skins of the kids, he attributes to the second source. The divine names and the peculiarities of language and style enable him to determine that the first source is J and the second E.

It is not necessary for us to examine, in all its details, the work of Gunkel, or that of the other commentators. It will suffice if we go over the verses seriatim, and endeavor to ascertain whether the analysis of the aforementioned scholars (paying special attention to that of Gunkel) is justified or not.

You are acquainted with the theme of the section. Two brothers, Jacob and Esau, contend with each other for their father's blessing, the blessing that belongs to the chosen son, who is destined to rule over his brother, as their mother had been told in the Lord's name at the time of her pregnancy: *and the one people shall be stronger than the other, and the elder shall serve the younger* (Gen. xxv 23). Which people would be the stronger of the two, we are not informed; which is the elder and which the younger is in doubt, since *the children struggled together within her* (*v.* 22) and they may have changed their relative positions as a result of their struggling. This aside, when they were born, Jacob came forth holding Esau's heel (*v.* 26), which shows that they had been striving with each other for primogeniture; and possibly they had then, if not earlier, interchanged their places. Nay more; the very oracle of the Lord could be interpreted to mean, though with difficulty, "the younger shall serve the elder." However, the words of Scripture: *Esau was a skillful hunter, a man of the field, while Jacob was a quiet man, dwelling in tents* (*v.* 27), as well as the whole tenor of the passage, clearly indicate that it is the intention of the Torah to inform us that the son worthy to receive his father's blessing and to continue Abraham's tradition was Jacob, not Esau.

But the narrative also leaves us with the impression that in the family circle the position was not so clear. Isaac, for instance, did not understand Jacob properly. Since "he ate of his game" (*v.* 28), Isaac's attitude towards Esau was marked by undue weakness, and this weakness induced in him a mental myopia that was far worse than his physical blindness. Only Rebekah his wife, with the alert intuition of a loving mother, understood who was deserving of seniority. In the case of Isaac, a reason is given for his affection: *because he ate of his game*; in Rebekah's case no motive is suggested—*but Rebekah loved Jacob* (*loc. cit.*), that is all. No explanation is needed, since her great love for Jacob stemmed from a full understanding of the character of her two sons, and not from some inherent psychological infirmity of hers.

As for the two brothers, it is self-understood that each one sought to interpret the words of the Lord in his own favor. But in order to secure to himself, also legally, the right that was due to him according to his personal interpretation, Jacob persuaded Esau to sell him his birthright (*vv*. 29-34). Notwithstanding, when the decisive moment arrived, the dispute between the two brothers broke out in all its virulence. Isaac did not budge from his view that the blessing still belonged to Esau, and Esau, who, at the time when the lentils were near at hand and the benison a long way off, had preferred the former, now that the lentils had long been forgotten and the benediction was about to be bestowed, refused to forgo the blessing. Hence the quarrel.

The first paragraph of the section (xxvii 1-4) relates how Isaac invited Esau to bring him some of his game and to receive his benison. *When Isaac was old and his eyes were dim so that he could not see* (the weakness of his physical sight was symbolic of the dimness of his mental vision, which still could not discern to whom the birthright belonged), *he called Esau, his older son, and said to him, 'My son'; and he answered, 'Here I am'* (*v*. 1). The words *and said to him, 'My son'; and he answered, 'Here I am'* are usually deleted, because the verse is attributed to J, and the use of such expressions in opening a conversation is characteristic of E.

But it is difficult to agree to this. Can such simple words be regarded as peculiar to any given writer and thus excluded from use by other authors? Furthermore, although such formulae are sometimes found in conjunction with the name ʾ*Elōhīm*, which is used only by E and not by J, yet they also occur in passages that contain no divine name at all, and they are found even in association with Yʜwʜ, which is characteristic of J; for instance in the verse: *But the angel of the* LORD [Yʜwʜ] *called to him from heaven, and said, 'Abraham, Abraham!' And he said, 'Here am I'* (xxii 11). The exponents of the documentary hypothesis omit the Tetragrammaton from this verse and substitute for it the name ʾ*Elōhīm*—an extremely easy method of enforcing textual conformity to any predetermined rule; and whenever this introductory formula appears in a paragraph that has no divine name, the passage is attributed to E on the basis of the rule that this opening is the private property of E, that is to say, on the strength of something that still has to be proved—a classic example of begging the question. Nor is this all; let us concede for a moment that the second part of the verse must be excised, then there remains only: *he called Esau, his older son, and said, 'Behold, I am old'*, etc. "And said"; to whom did he say? The text should have read אֵלָיו ʾ*ēlāw* ["to him"]. The absence of the word ʾ*ēlāw* in xxvii 2 establishes beyond doubt that the sentence is not the beginning of the conversation, and that we have no right to omit the first part of the conversation recorded in the preceding verse. Had these opening words been wanting, we should have had to supply them.

In verses 2-4 it is stated: *He said, 'Behold, I am old; I do not know the day of my death. Now then, take your weapons, your quiver and your bow, and go out to the field, and hunt game for me, and prepare for me savory food, such as I love, and bring it to me that I may eat; that I may bless you before I die.'* The words *and prepare for me savory food... that I may eat* are likewise deleted and attributed to E on the ground that two different, but parallel, motifs are mentioned here, that of *game* and that of *savory food*, pointing to two recensions of the story. The motif of *savory food*, which is connected with the skins of the kids, is assigned to E, and that of the *game* to J.

Is this correct? Let us now examine what is left in each of the two documents after the division. To J there remains: *Now then, take your weapons, your quiver and your bow, and go out to the field, and hunt game for me, that I may bless you before I die.* The essential point is missing from the text. It is not enough that Esau should hunt game in some place far from his father's home; the important thing is that he should bring the game home, and prepare food from it for his father, and hand the food to him. And what is left to E? *And he said to him, 'My son'; and he answered, 'Here I am.' He said, 'Prepare for me savory food, such as I love, and bring it to me that I may eat.'* This is even more bizarre. Is the valiant Esau, the skillful hunter, the man of the field, to be transformed into a kind of housewife, who prepares savory dishes on the stove? The passage as we have it in its complete form is well and clearly arranged; it is lucid and fully comprehensible to the reader. But each of its segments, ascribed to one source or another, is but a crude torso, without sense or meaning.

Esau immediately hastens to go forth into the field to hunt and bring back game. Rebekah, who overheard what her husband enjoined him, is troubled by the matter and ponders how to rectify the error. To dissuade Isaac, who remains inflexible with an old man's obduracy, is unthinkable; how much more so, to influence Esau. Then what is to be done? There is no alternative—so she thinks—but to have recourse to guile. She will prepare savory food as Isaac loves, and Jacob will bring it to his blind father and say that he is Esau back from his hunting, and thus he will receive his father's blessing instead of his brother. Therein Rebekah sinned and caused Jacob to sin, as I have explained on another occasion. It is true that the benison was rightly due to Jacob, but for that very reason they should have eschewed any deceitful deed; they should have trusted in the Lord—that He would act.

Also this, the second paragraph (*vv.* 5-10) is divided between the two documents. To J is ascribed all that is written as far as, and including, the words *bring me game* (*v.* 7); to E is assigned all that follows, beginning with the words *and prepare for me savory food* and ending with *so that he may bless you before he dies* (end of *v.* 10). The game is referred to J and the savory food to E. It is true that in E's part the Tetragrammaton occurs (*v.* 7), but, if the text militates against the theory, alas for the text! The remedy is at hand: the words *before* YHWH in *v.* 7 are deleted, and everything is in order.

But, no! everything is not in order. One observation is enough to upset the apple cart completely. In the opening words of Rebekah, in the portion ascribed to J, we find: *Behold* [הִנֵּה *hinnē*], *I heard your father*, etc. (*v.* 6), and in the continuation, in the portion attributed to E, we read: *Now therefore* [וְעַתָּה *weʿattā*], *my son, obey my word*, etc. (*v.* 8). The two expressions *hinnē* and *weʿattā* are interconnected in the structure of Hebrew speech and constitute a *pair* of words [correlatives] that cannot be separated. The word *hinnē* introduces the premise and *weʿattā* the conclusion flowing therefrom, and it is impossible to have the premise without the conclusion and *vice versa*. If a corroborative illustration of this usage is needed, we have not to look far for our evidence. In our own section we read: BEHOLD [*hinnē*], *I am old; I do not know the day of my death.* Now THEN [*weʿattā*], *take up your weapons*, etc. (*vv.* 2-3). It is manifest, therefore, that the beginning of Rebekah's utterance must not be divorced from the end, just as the two parts of a pair of scissors are not to be detached, for neither blade cuts so long as it remains disconnected from the other.

Let us now proceed to the third paragraph (*vv.* 11-17). Jacob hesitates. He does not doubt that the privilege of the blessing is his by right, nor is he deterred—and herein lies his chief transgression—by the deception involved. He is only afraid lest his father should recognize him and he would *seem to him as a mocker* (*v.* 12). *As a mocker*, he says, not *a mocker*, and only *seem to him*, not in actuality. This expression—resembling as it does the statement about Lot: *But he* SEEMED *to his sons-in-law to be jesting* [literally, "as one who jests"] (xix 14), when in fact he was speaking with complete earnestness—is so worded that we may understand that it did not appear to Jacob that what his mother counselled him to do was in truth an act of mockery, since, in the final analysis, he was going to take what was due to him. Nevertheless, the Torah rightly condemned his action, as we noted earlier in this course of lectures. The end does not justify the means.

Finally, when his mother urges him, he sets aside all his doubts and hastens to do her bidding. The short words that follow each other in succession (xxvii 13-14: *and go fetch me* [them]. *So he went and fetched* [them] *and brought* [them] *to his mother*) and the repetition of the verbs (*go fetch—so he went and fetched*) are expressive of the swiftness of the action and the exactness with which Rebekah's instructions were carried out. The danger lest Isaac should recognize Jacob, Rebekah seeks to overcome by dressing Jacob in Esau's garments, and by covering his hands and the smooth part of his neck with the skins of kids. These two devices—the clothes and the skins—the commentators consider, as I have already stated, to be unmistakable signs of two versions; and so they have also divided this, the third paragraph, between the two documents.

However, the two stratagems do not conflict. On the contrary, they are necessary to each other. It is usual for a blind person to make good his lack of sight by means of the other senses—by means of *all* the other senses. Seeing that Esau differed from his brother in respect of the hair that covered his body and the odor of the fields that clung to his garments, it was but natural that Jacob and Rebekah should pay heed to the dangers arising from touch and smell simultaneously. Nay more; the two remaining senses also come into play in our narrative: the sense of taste in regard to the savory food, which Rebekah undoubtedly prepared in a special way so that the flesh of the kids—domestic animals— should resemble that of wild animals; and the sense of hearing in connection with Isaac's remark: *The voice is Jacob's voice* (v. 22), for apparently Jacob tried, though without much success, to imitate Esau's voice. Therefore, if we were to divide the section according to the senses mentioned therein, we should have to discover in it not two but four sources.

Another point: there is an objection to the division of this paragraph that is decisive. It is stated: *and the skins of the kids she put* [הִלְבִּישָׁה *hilbīšā*] *upon his hands*, etc. (v. 16). Why is not the verb here at the beginning of the sentence and in the imperfect with *wāw* conversive, as is usual in scriptural narratives? Why is it not written: "and she put [וַתַּלְבֵּשׁ *wattalbēš*] the skins of the kids upon his hands," etc.? We shall understand the construction of this verse if we compare similar instances in biblical narrative prose. When a verb occurs twice in parallel succession, the Bible is accustomed to change its tense and position: once it appears in the imperfect converted to the past, and subsequently in the perfect; the first time it comes at the beginning of the sentence, and the second time, after some other word. Thus we find, for example: *And God* CALLED [וַיִּקְרָא *wayyiqrā*] *the light Day, and the darkness* HE CALLED [קָרָא *qārā*] *Night* (i 5). In the story of Cain and Abel we read: *Now Abel* WAS [וַיְהִי *wayehī*] *a keeper of sheep, and Cain* WAS [הָיָה *hāyā*] *a tiller of the ground* (iv 2); and later: *Cain* BROUGHT [וַיָּבֵא *wayyābhē*] *of the fruit of the ground an offering to the Lord, and Abel, too, brought* [הֵבִיא *hēbhī*], etc. (vv. 3-4); and again: *And the Lord* HAD REGARD [וַיִּשַׁע *wayyiša*] *for Abel and his offering, but for Cain and his offering* HE HAD *no* REGARD [שָׁעָה *šāʿā*] (*vv.* 4-5). In the story of the Generation of Division (i.e., Tower of Babel) it is written: *And they* HAD [וַתְּהִי *watehī*] *brick for stone, and bitumen* HAD [הָיָה *hāyā*] *they for mortar* (xi 3). So we may continue to quote, but there is no need to cite further examples. In the present instance, also, we find *hilbīšā* and not *wattalbēš*; and the verb does not come at the beginning of the sentence, because in the previous verse, the very verse that is detached from its context and assigned to another source, the form *wattalbēš* occurs. *Wattalbēš–hilbīšā* corresponds exactly to *wayyiqrā'–qārā', wayehī–hāyā, wayyabhē'–hēbhī', wayyiša'–šā'ā, wattehī–hāyā*. Thus it is clear that when the two verses were first written they were already linked together; hence they cannot be separated.

After Rebekah had prepared the savory food, Jacob immediately hastened—so the fourth paragraph (xxvii 18-20) tells us—to take it in his hand and to bring it to his father. At first Isaac was doubtful about his identity, but after he had heard his replies to his questions, and had felt his hairy hands, he was convinced that his son Esau was in truth standing before him, and he bestowed his blessing upon him. This paragraph, too, the principal paragraph of our section, is, like the preceding paragraphs, divided between J and E. It is possible, indeed, that anyone reading it superficially and hastily will gain the impression here and there, particularly from the verses containing the dialogue between Isaac and Jacob, that the passage suffers from a certain redundancy of words. But the careful reader will come to no such conclusion. Every word is weighed, every utterance of the conversation is in its right and proper place.

The duologue opens with expressions that recall the earlier conversation between Isaac and Esau: *So he went to his father, and said, 'My father'; and he said, 'Here I am'* (*v.* 18). This was not the denouement envisaged by Isaac when he said to Esau, "My son," and he answered, "Here I am." From the parallelism of words and the antithesis of events we begin to grasp the tragedy of the

situation. How great is the gulf between Isaac's original plan and
what was happening now! How wretched is the plight of the old
father, who, enveloped in darkness despite the brightness of the
day, has no means of realizing this vast disparity! Who then is
it that is calling me "My father"? It is certainly one of my two
sons, and his voice is undoubtedly that of one of the twins; but
of which of them? The voice resembles Jacob's more, but I am
awaiting Esau's coming. Who then is it? Such was the tragic doubt
in Isaac's mind at the moment that was so fateful for the life of
his sons and later descendants. To rid himself of this doubt, he
has no alternative but to ask a question; and since the two pos-
sibilities are equally probable, he frames his question in noncom-
mittal form: *who are you, my son?* (*v.* 18).

The inquiry certainly does not come as a surprise to Jacob.
He begins his answer with: I [אָנֹכִי *ʾānōkhī*] *am Esau your firstborn*
(*v.* 19). You will recall that we discussed the difference between
the pronouns אֲנִי *ʾănī* and אָנֹכִי *ʾānōkhī* ["I"], and we saw that
whenever the predicate was a noun and not a verb, *ʾānōkhī* was
used, if it was intended to give greater emphasis to the subject; and
conversely *ʾănī* occurred when it was desired to stress the predicate.
Hence, when a speaker introduces himself and says who he is, giving his name, the pronoun is, as a rule, *ʾănī*, because the emphasis
falls on the predicate, for instance: I [*ʾănī*] *am Joseph*; I [*ʾănī*] *am
God Almighty*; I [*ʾănī*] *am the Lord.* But here the identification is
false, and in spite of himself Jacob cannot emphasize the name
that is not his. The name seems to sear his lips, and ineluctably
he stresses the pronoun more and says *ʾānōkhī*. On the other hand,
when the real Esau enters later and presents himself without any
fear or hesitation, he says forthwith: I [*ʾănī*] *am your son, your firstborn, Esau* (*v.* 32), employing the usual pronoun *ʾănī*.

After identifying himself, Jacob continues: *I have done as you
told me* (*v.* 19)—a vague statement such as would be made by
a person who is compelled, in consequence of his previous lies,

to speak about a subject with which he is not fully conversant, and he is afraid that if he goes into details he will be caught out. Only when he proceeds to the remaining part of his speech does Jacob feel that he is on sure ground, and then his words flow freely: *now sit up and eat of my game, that you may bless me* (ibid.). Nevertheless, Isaac cannot rest; the position is still not quite clear to him. It is true that the man standing before him did say that he was Esau his firstborn, but he did not say it convincingly. That apart, his voice still seems more like Jacob's than Esau's. Furthermore, how did Esau contrive to be so quick? Doubts multiply and grow stronger in Isaac's mind. Once again he attempts to resolve his perplexity by means of a question. Now he is able to inquire more specifically than at first, since the answer he had been given, *I am Esau your firstborn, I have done as you told me*, favors Esau. Hence, he bases his query on the premise that it is actually Esau who is before him: *How is it that you have found it so quickly, my son?* (*v.* 19). He hopes that the reply will dispel simultaneously both doubts that trouble him: it will explain the extreme quickness of his return, and it will also enable him to hear the voice of the speaker, thus affording him a further opportunity of recognizing him by the intonation of his speech.

In truth, it is difficult for Jacob to find an adequate answer to this question. What can he say, seeing that he is not "a skillful hunter" and knows nothing at all about hunting? Once more he can reply only in general terms: *Because the Lord your God granted me success* (ibid.). Possibly his words also contain an allusion to himself—to soothe his conscience, as it were—hinting that it was Providence that had so directed the course of events that in the end the blessing might come to him. But such a rejoinder that gives us a glimpse of the speaker's perplexity, and is conveyed in a voice that still resembles Jacob's rather than Esau's, did not suffice to put Isaac's mind at ease. The situation becomes increasingly dramatic: on the one hand we see the aged father endeavoring desperately to tear asunder the veil that hides the truth from him; and on the other, his son taken in the toils of his own falsehoods, which, even as he casts about for a way of escape, grow tighter around him.

Now Isaac realizes that by question and answer he will not succeed in clarifying the matter, and he tries another way, which, he believes, will allow of no error, namely, the sense of touch: *Come near, that I may feel you, my son, to know whether you are really my son Esau or not* (v. 21). The tension now reaches its climax; we seem to hear the beating of the two hearts as we read: *So Jacob went near to Isaac his father; and he felt him* (v. 22). At this point the Torah appears to realize our need for release from much prolonged tension, and immediately hastens to inform us: *And he did not recognize him, because his hands were hairy like his brother Esau's hands; so he blessed him* (v. 23).

"So he blessed him." How he blessed him the Bible tells us later. The tension is abated; quietly and calmly we are given the remaining particulars of the central theme of the section—the details of the blessing. First, a preamble: a kind of declaration by Isaac that it is actually Esau who is standing before him (*Are you really my son Esau?*—v. 24); this is intended, as it were, to banish any lingering doubt from his mind by his own admission and to elicit a final affirmative answer from his son, an affirmation that Jacob gives as though under demonic compulsion in one brief word: ʾănī [*I am*] (since the predicate Esau is not expressly stated, but is only inferred from its previous mention by the question—and consequently the reply contains the pronoun only—Jacob, who cannot stress his deceptive reply, uses here the pronominal form that is customary when there is no intention to emphasize it). We then come to the next stage, the acceptance and eating of the savory food from the son's hands (v. 25). The third stage is reached when the father invites his son to come near to him and kiss him and receive his blessing (*v.* 26). Finally, we have the wording of the blessing.

The father's request to the son, *Come near and kiss me* (ibid.), is not to be regarded as another attempt by Isaac to identify his son by the sense of smell, as most modern expositors think. This attempt would have been too late now, since Isaac had already accepted the savory food and eaten it. He had to ask his son to draw near to him so that he might place his hand on him; a benison cannot be given from afar. The odor of Esau's clothes reaches Isaac without his having intended it, and provides corroboration—which is all the more important since it was unsolicited—of something of which he is already certain, to wit, that his firstborn son was standing before him. By this means Scripture reminds us of Esau's garments, which Rebekah had put on Jacob, a detail that we had almost forgotten, and links it up artistically with the course of the narrative; at the same time the reference to the smell of the garments serves to prepare the way for the opening words of the blessing: *See, the* SMELL *of my son is as the* SMELL *of a field which the Lord has blessed* (*v.* 27).

But, you may argue, this detailed narration, after we have already been told, *Then he blessed him* (*v.* 23), constitutes a duplication and indicates a composite text. No! this is another example of the literary technique of first making a general statement and following it up with a particularized description, which, as we have noted, is a common feature of the pentateuchal stories. Above, the Bible rightly made a simple reference to the fact that the blessing was given, in order, as we have explained, to reduce the tension, and to make it possible for the tranquil and formal account of the details to be given in a relaxed atmosphere.

As for the benediction itself, one can adduce numerous arguments in support of its unity and against its division between the two sources. I shall not detail them all here. To one of them, however—the most typical—I shall refer briefly. It is as follows: the wording of the blessing bestowed here on Jacob contains, like the blessing vouchsafed to Abraham (xii 2-3) and that given to Isaac (xxvi 3-4, from *and I will be with you* up to *all the nations of the earth*), *seven* expressions of benison: one in xxvii 28 and six in xxvii 29 (every verb constituting a separate benediction). Seven is the number of perfection, and each of the three patriarchs received a perfect blessing, a sevenfold benison.

Thus we find that also this, the fourth paragraph, contains no redundancy or discrepancy whatsoever. On the contrary, it affords a classic example of outstandingly beautiful narrative art, and by dismembering it we only destroy a wonderful literary work, the like of which it is hard to find.

Is there any need to continue our investigation? I think not. It seems to me superfluous to repeat to you all that I have already published on the rest of our section, as well as on the other sections that are likewise held to be composite. The ground that we have covered suffices to establish the character and effectiveness of the method of documentary analysis, and to point the way to a new exegetical approach capable of replacing it. It is evident that the fifth pillar, like its companions, is also without substance.

CONCLUSIONS

THE TOUR OF INSPECTION on which I invited you to ac-
company me during this course has come to an end. We must
now retrace our steps and review the results achieved by our tour.
To this review I propose to devote today's lecture—the concluding lecture of this series.

There stood before us an imposing edifice, accounted one of
the most important and durable of contemporary scholarship, the
structure of the documentary hypothesis. Those who built and
perfected it, and are still busy decorating its halls and completing its turrets, were proud of it. But latterly there have arisen a
few among them who have criticized one or another detail of its
plan. They have argued, for example, that the design of this hall
or that tower should be altered; or that a certain window should
be closed or a new one opened in its place, and so on. Yet they
have not dared to touch the main lineaments of its pattern. It
seemed as though this structure could still endure for generations. *Wisdom has built her house*, as the biblical poet sang, *she
has hewn her seven pillars* (Prov. ix 1). Although in the present

instance the house rested on five pillars and not on seven, as did Wisdom of old, yet the five pillars upheld the building in all its strength and glory.

So it seemed. But we did not permit the splendor of the edifice to blind us, nor did we allow the profound impression it apparently made on those who gazed upon it to mislead us; we decided to enter it with open eyes in order to test its stability and to probe the nature and value of the five pillars on which it rested.

We started with the first pillar, the variations in the use of the divine names, and a detailed study of the subject showed us that these changes depended on the primary signification of the Names and on the rules governing their use in life and literature, rules that applied to the entire body of biblical literature and even to post-biblical Hebrew writings, and are rooted in the literary traditions common to the peoples of the ancient East. Since we saw that these factors fully solved the problem of the changing of the divine names—leaving nothing unexplained—on the basis of principles that are radically different from those of the documentary theory, we came to the conclusion that the first pillar is void of substance.

We then approached the second pillar, the inequalities of language and style, of which we examined the most important examples. As a result of this investigation we found that these linguistic disparities, insofar as they really existed, could be explained with the utmost simplicity by reference to the general rules of the language, its grammatical structure, its lexical usages, and its literary conventions—general rules that applied equally to every Hebrew writer and every Hebrew book. We thus saw that in this respect, too, there was no question of different documents, and that the second pillar was only an empty delusion.

Thereafter, we probed the third pillar, the differences in the subject matter of the sections. We made a study of some of the most significant and typical instances of these divergences, and

we learnt that where there were actual discrepancies between the
sections, they were not of a kind that could not be found in
a homogeneous work. On the contrary, such incongruities were
inevitable in a multi-faceted book like the one before us, which
contains materials of varied origin and character, and consequently presents its themes from different viewpoints. Hence we
concluded that the third pillar was also incapable of withstand-
ing criticism.

After this, we proceeded to the fourth pillar, the duplications
and repetitions. We considered classical illustrations of each of
these categories, and we clearly saw, as a result of our study, that
underlying both of them was a specific intention, which not only
was reflected in the final redaction of the sections but was evident
even in their original composition. We consequently decided that
the fourth pillar was not stronger than the preceding three.

Finally, we turned our attention to the fifth pillar, the composite sections. For the purpose of investigating the conventional
theory regarding the division of these sections, we examined in
detail one of the most characteristic examples of this analysis, and
we realized that this hypothesis relied on evidence that in truth
did not point to a composite text; on the contrary, exact study
revealed unmistakable and conclusive indications of a close connection between the parts of the section that were considered to
belong to different sources. From all this, we judged the last pillar to be likewise without foundation.

I also added that apart from what we observed together in the
course of this tour, a more comprehensive and detailed inspection
of all the relevant material could be made in my company by those
who would study my Italian work *La Questione della Genesi* on
this subject. But I believe that the main conclusions that we have
stated have been amply demonstrated and made clear to you.

But now what is the principle that emerges from these
conclusions?

Since we saw in the first lecture that the whole structure of the documentary hypothesis rested on the five pillars enumerated, and subsequently we found that all these pillars were without substance, it follows that this imposing and beautiful edifice has, in reality, nothing to support it and is founded on air.

However, one of the critics of my book argued that my contentions were not conclusive because the structure of the hypothesis was upheld not by each pillar separately but by their combined strength, and that the views of the exponents of the documentary theory were based on the total effect created by all the evidence taken together. But this stricture is easily answered. If I had only shown that the pillars were weak and that not one of them was a decisive support, then the argument would have been valid; and in the past it was rightly used by the adherents of the dominant theory in rebuttal of the partial criticisms levelled by other scholars against their hypothesis. Although each pillar by itself was unable to carry the weight of the entire building, possibly they could do so unitedly. However, the evidence that I adduced went much further. I demonstrated not that it was *possible* to solve the problems in a different way from that of the documentary theory, but that they *must* be resolved differently, and that it was *impossible* to find a solution on the basis of this doctrine. I did not prove that the pillars were weak or that each one failed to give decisive support, but I established that they were not pillars at all, that they did not exist, that they were purely imaginary. In view of this, my final conclusion that the documentary hypothesis is null and void is justified. If you wish to draw a heavy cart by means of a rope, and the rope you have is too frail for the task, it is certainly of help to twine two or three similar cords together, so that jointly they may be strong enough to draw the wagon; but if you have no real ropes but only figments of the imagination, even a thousand of them will not avail you to move the cart from its place. The sum of nought plus nought plus nought *ad infinitum* is only nought.

But should you ask what kind of structure in biblical scholarship would be capable of taking the place of the documentary theory, which has not stood the test of our criticism, I must tell you, friends, that to answer this question requires an entire series of lectures, and the answer cannot therefore be given at the end of this lecture. Furthermore, the new edifice has not yet been completed, and it is not possible to describe something that is nonexistent. Nevertheless what I have stated so far already points to certain features in the design of the new building that I visualize.

I have, on several occasions, referred to the fact that there were undoubtedly current among the Israelites, before the Torah was written, numerous traditions relating to the beginning of the world's history and the earliest generations, to the fathers of the Hebrew nation and to what befell them.[1] Without doubt these traditions were far more extensive than those that were actually incorporated in the Torah. In Scripture itself we find a number of passing allusions to matters that are not specifically dealt with. We are told, for instance, at the end of the story of the Garden of Eden: *and at the east of the Garden of Eden He placed the cherubim, and the sword-flame which turned every way, to guard the way to the tree of life* (Gen. iii 24). Since "the cherubim" and "the sword-flame which turned every way" have the definite article, it is clear that the forefathers of Israel were familiar with them. So, too, the statement with regard to Enoch, *And Enoch walked with God, and he was not; for God took him* (v 24), refers to miraculous events, which are not detailed in the passage. Haran is described as *the father of Milcah and the father of Iscah* (xi 29), indicating that Milcah and Iscah were well-known, although Iscah is mentioned nowhere else in the Bible, and concerning Milcah we have only a few genealogical notices. The following allusion brings out the point even more clearly: *he is Anah who found the hot springs in the wilderness, as he pastured the asses of Zibeon his father* (xxxvi 24). It would be easy to enlarge still further on the matter and to cite many more verses that testify to the existence of numerous sagas among the Israelites before the Torah came to be written; but those we have mentioned will suffice for the present. We would only add that the rabbinic sages were of the same opinion, for they tell us that, when the children of Israel were in bondage under Pharaoh, they possessed many scrolls in which they found pleasure Sabbath by Sabbath (Shemoth Rabba v 22).

It is no daring conjecture, therefore, to suppose that a whole world of traditions was known to the Israelites in olden times, traditions that apparently differed in their origin, nature and characteristics. Some of them preserved memories of ancient events, and some belonged to the category of folklore; some were the product of the Israelite spirit and some contained elements that emanated from pagan culture; a number of them were handed down by the general populace and others were subjected to the close study of the exponents of the wisdom literature; there were stories that were given a poetic and consequently more fixed form, and others that were narrated in prose that was liable to suffer changes in the course of time; there were simple tales and complex, succinct and detailed, lucid and obscure, unpretentious and most sublime. From all this treasure, the Torah selected those traditions that appeared suited to its aims, and then proceeded to purify and refine them, to arrange and integrate them, to recast their style and phrasing, and generally to give them a new aspect of its own design, until they were welded into a unified whole.

Of the elements that were not accepted, some sank slowly into oblivion and were completely lost. But others continued to exist for generations, and although in the course of time their form changed considerably—they were elaborated or emasculated, and much new material was grafted on them—nevertheless they were preserved in the Jewish national tradition till a late date. The stream of this tradition may be compared to a great and wide-spreading river that traverses vast distances; although in the course of its journey the river loses part of its water, which is absorbed by the ground or evaporates in the air because of the heat of the sun, and it is also increasingly augmented by the waters of the tributaries that pour into it, yet it carries with it, even after it has covered hundreds of miles, some of the waters that it held at the beginning when it first started to flow from its original source. In its upper course, among the high mountains, its waters formed themselves into a divine pool, wondrous and enchanting, in which the blue heavens are reflected: this is our Book of Genesis. In its lower reaches in the plain, it created other delightful pools, like the Book of Jubilees or Bereshith Zuṭa, and still lower down—Bereshith Rabba.

With the help of this theory we can find a solution to the problems connected with the narratives of the Torah. It also opens for us the way to the solution of the questions appertaining to its statutes. Obviously it is impossible for us now, at the last moment, to touch upon this type of problem, with which we have not dealt at all throughout our lectures. But this at least may be stated: the results of the new hypothesis relative to the penta-teuchal stories will serve, in the same way as did the conclusions of the documentary theory concerning these narratives, as a basis and guide for research in the legal sphere.

To this we may add something else at this stage—be it only by way of a cursory reference, since we are nearing the end of this, the final lecture, and there is no time to elaborate—something with regard to the general character of the new edifice that is to be built in place of the old, collapsed structure, to wit, that in two principal aspects, in particular, the second building will differ from the first.

The first will be the tendency to recognize the unity of the Torah—a unity, in truth, that does not exclude, as you have heard, a multiplicity and variety of source materials, or even their reflection in the text before us; but a unity, nonetheless. The Jewish people is one throughout the world, despite the many differences between its members, who belong to various communities, places of abode and groupings; the same applies to books. Suffice it to mention, if I may revert again to the illustration I cited from Italian literature, the *Divina Commedia* of Dante Alighieri. Dante derived his material from the Christian tradition and Greek and Roman culture, from the Hebrew Bible and the New Testament and the works of the classical poets and thinkers, from contemporary science and popular folklore, from philosophical speculation and the concepts of the populace, from historical records and the living trends of his environment, from the antagonisms between the states and the strife among the factions, from the contemplation of nature and reflection on the mystery of God's existence. The multi-faceted character of the sources from which he drew his material is reflected in his poetry, which contains the dramatic and very graphic descriptions of the "Inferno" and the doctrinal discourses of the "Paradiso," and varies its style and phraseology from passage to passage with the change of subject, using, as occasion requires, harsh words or dulcet tones, sentences sharp as a double-edged sword and others that are sweeter than honey. Despite all this, the poet left on the whole of this variegated material the unmistakable impress of his wonderful spirit, and succeeded in transforming the chaos of the conglomeration of sources into a perfect, unique harmony, and in fusing all the separate elements into a homogeneous work of art. This is the peculiar attribute of great books that what they take from their sources receives in them a new form; it is integrated, knit together and unified as the author deems fit.* It is impossible

---

* "As the author deems fit." The Hebrew, which is quoted from Jer. xviii 4, literally means: *as it seemed good to the potter to do.*

for the scholar to solve the problem of their sources without paying heed to the added element, since apart from the material deriving from the sources, and transcending it, there exists something that no investigator can probe, the enigma of the soul of the writer and the mystery of the burgeoning of his literary work.

The second characteristic—in this respect, too, a few words will suffice, since I discussed the subject at length in an essay that I wrote in Hebrew seven years ago[2]—will be the determination of the relative chronology of the Pentateuch and the prophetic writings. The latter did not precede the Torah, as the generally accepted view of our day maintains, but *vice versa*. The precedence is not chronological only, as Yeḥezkel Kaufman supposes, taking the view that although the Pentateuch was written before the prophetical works, they "are two polarically different domains." In my view they constitute rather a single sequence. The divergences between them are explicable on the basis of the difference in their content, aim and orientation. The laws and regulations of any association differ in character from the propaganda addresses of its leaders and the critical speeches that are delivered at the meetings of its members; nevertheless both are the product of the same spirit. So, too, one spirit moves the Torah and prophecy. Prophetic literature has its roots in the pentateuchal literature, from which it draws its sustenance. Even the oldest of the "literary prophets," Amos and Hosea—the prophets of righteousness and love, respectively—at no time proclaim new ideals or concepts or beliefs, and this is true *a fortiori* of those who came after them. The prophets speak of their ideals and concepts and beliefs as of principles with which their listeners are already quite familiar. They rebuke their brethren for not acting according to these tenets, or for not understanding them properly, or for drawing wrong conclusions from them; and they teach them how to conduct themselves in accordance with these ideals, how to understand them, how to draw the necessary inferences from them; but they never claim to have created new doctrines or laws. Moreover, it is manifest from their prophecies that no such thought occurred to them, nor was it possible for their audiences to have entertained such an idea. When we examine their speeches without any preconceived ideas, we see clearly that their words can be explained only on the premise that prophecy developed on the foundation of the Torah writings.

These, if I do not err, will be the principal features of the new edifice that the biblical scholars of our generation are called upon to erect.

BIBLIOGRAPHICAL NOTES

AS I STATED IN THE PREFACE, I append here a few brief bibliographical notes for the guidance of those who wish to make a deeper study of the problems dealt with in these lectures. In order not to make the bibliography unduly long, I shall not actually give a detailed list of books, but I shall indicate where the reader can find the information. In addition, I shall mention some of the literature on the subject that has recently appeared in Hebrew.

My Italian work, *La Questione della Genesi*, which treats at length the topics that this little volume discusses in summarized form, I shall hereafter quote as QG.

GENERAL NOTE. A full bibliography on problems considered here and on related questions, the reader will find in QG, pp. 401-409 (List of Abbreviations) and in the footnotes throughout the book; also in Y. Kaufman's תּוֹלְדוֹת הָאֱמוּנָה הַיִּשְׂרְאֵלִית *Tōledhōth Hāʾĕmūnā Hayyiśrĕʾēlīth*, Tel Aviv 1936, i, pp. 11-17, and in the footnotes in the rest of the book. Recent publications are listed particularly in two scientific periodicals that devote considerable space to bibliography. These are (a) the German periodical *Zeitschrift für die alttestamentliche Wissenschaft*, which gives in almost every issue a list of *articles* in the field of biblical scholarship that appeared in other publications, adding as a rule a synopsis of their content; indexes, arranged according to subjects [*Sachregister*] and according to biblical texts [*Stellenregister*], respectively, are included every year in its last issue, thus facilitating the reader's use of the bibliography; (b) the periodical *Biblica*, which is published under the auspices of the Pontifical Biblical Institute in Rome and gives each year a list of new *books* and *essays* relating to biblical research. The bibliography is arranged according to subjects and is distributed over the four parts that appear annually; at the end of the last part there is an index of authors.

PREFACE

1. *La Questione della Genesi*, Florence 1934, iii Serie, vol. i.

LECTURE I

1. A history of the documentary theory, from Astruc (the first attempt in this direction by Witter was still buried in oblivion) till about twenty years ago, as well as bibliographical information about the most important works on the subject, is to be found in the book by M. Soloveichik and Z. Rubashov, תּוֹלְדוֹת בִּקֹרֶת הַמִּקְרָא *Tōledōth Biqqōreth Hammiqrā'*, Berlin 1925, pp. 65-122. For the more recent period the reader can consult the bibliographies in the two periodicals mentioned above, in the *General Note*.

2. On the attempts to solve our problems by methods different from those employed by the documentary hypothesis, and for the relevant bibliography, see QG, pp. 5-16.

3. On the *statutes of the Torah*, see Y. Kaufman, *op. cit.*, i, pp. 47-80, and *passim*; his notes contain a detailed bibliography. A few months ago there appeared the following Hebrew book dealing specifically with the pentateuchal laws: D. and M. Avidov (Gershman), נְתִיבוֹת בְּבִקֹּרֶת הַמִּקְרָא *Nethībhōth*

Bᵉbhiqqōreth Hammiqrā' [Tel Aviv 1940]; see my review of it in *Kirjath Sepher*, xviii (1941), p. 7.

LECTURE 2

1. The first chapter of *La Questione della Genesi*, pp. 1-92, is devoted to this subject; a complete bibliography is given in the notes. The Hebrew reader will find a selected bibliography on the same subject at the end of my article שְׁמוֹת הָאֱלֹהִים בַּמִּקְרָא *"Sᵉmōth Hā'elōhīm bammiqrā',"* in the Jewish Encyclopedia אֶשְׁכּוֹל *'Eškōl*, Hebrew edition, ii, pp. 453-454 (German edition, vii, p. 559).

2. This view was expressed by my respected colleague Prof. M.H. Segal in his article הַשֵּׁמוֹת יי ואלֹהִים בְּסִפְרֵי הַמִּקְרָא *"Haššēmōth* Yʜwʜ *Wᵉ'lōhīm bᵉsiphrē hammiqrā',"* *Tarbiz*, ix (1938), pp. 123-163. The writer argues against the views I expressed in QG; at times he fails to understand my contentions correctly, and raises objections that have no bearing on the real meaning of what I wrote. I intend to revert to this subject in detail elsewhere.

LECTURE 3

1. The continuation of the investigation to the end of Genesis and the beginning of Exodus will be found in QG, pp. 49-60, 82-92. There (pp. 60-82) I also discuss at length the names אֵל *'El* and שַׁדַּי *Šadday*; a detailed bibliography is given in the footnotes. See also below, the note on pp. 60-62.

LECTURE 4

1. This subject is dealt with in detail in the second chapter of QG, pp. 93-178. A bibliography on the lists of linguistic and stylistic variations mentioned here on p. 51, is given in QG, p. 93, note 1. A comprehensive bibliography on the entire subject will be found there in the notes on the whole chapter.

LECTURE 5

1. The third chapter of QG, pp. 179-254, is devoted to this subject. A list of publications on the current views on the subject is given *ibid.*, p. 179, note 1. A full bibliography on the whole subject is to be found in the notes in the continuation of the chapter.

2. See now Prof. Segal's article, גִּלּוּיוֹ שֶׁל שֵׁם הֲוָיָה "*Gillūyō šel šem Hāwāyā,*" *Tarbiz,* xii (1941), pp. 97-108. I am particularly pleased that my colleague's views correspond in the main with those that I have expressed in QG, pp. 82-92.

LECTURE 6

1. I deal with this subject in detail in QG, chapter iv, pp. 255-318, where a detailed bibliography will be found in the notes. The investigation of the duplications and repetitions in accordance with the documentary theory reached its climax in the book by O. Eissfeldt, *Hexateuch-Synopse,* Leipzig 1922, which I cite in QG, p. 156, note 1. I mention the detailed studies of Allgeier and Schulz *ibid.*, pp. 401, 408.

LECTURE 7

1. I discuss this subject in QG, chapter v, pp. 319-391; an extensive bibliography will be found there in the notes. In regard, also, to the composition of the sections see especially Eissfeldt, *op. cit.*

On the chronological difficulties that have lent support to the documentary theory see QG, pp. 374-381; those connected with the story of Tamar and Judah I have discussed in a special essay in Hebrew, in צִיּוּנִים *Ṣiyyūnīm,* Memorial Volume dedicated to J.N. Simḥoni, Berlin 1929, pp. 93-100.

LECTURE 8

1. On my views concerning the sources of the Torah see QG, pp. 393-398.

2. This essay, entitled הוֹשֵׁעַ הַנָּבִיא וְסִפְרֵי הַתּוֹרָה "Hōšēʿa hannābhī wᵉsiphrē Hattōrā," was published in Maʾāmārīm, Memorial Volume dedicated to Zebi Perez Chajes, Vienna 1933, Hebrew section, pp. 262-275. See also my article הַפֶּרֶק הַשֵּׁנִי בְּסֵפֶר הוֹשֵׁעַ "Happereq haššēnī bᵉsēpher Hōšēʿa," Memorial Volume in honor of Dr. Samuel Abraham Poznanski, Warsaw 1927, Hebrew Section, pp. 115-135.

INDEX OF BIBLICAL REFERENCES

INDEX